SOMETHING *of* INSIDE *Me*

HOW TO HANG ON TO HEAVEN
WHEN YOU'RE GOING THROUGH HELL

CHITOKA WEBB

EMERALD
BOOK CO.

This memoir is a factual account according to the author's recollections. Some names and identifying details have been changed in order to protect the privacy of individuals.

Published by Emerald Book Company
Austin, TX
www.emeraldbookcompany.com

Distributed by Emerald Book Company

For ordering information or special discounts for bulk purchases, please contact Emerald Book Company at PO Box 91869, Austin, TX 78709, 512.891.6100.

Design and composition by Greenleaf Book Group LLC
Cover design by Jay Arnold, iDesign Inc. www.iDesignInc.net
& Greenleaf Book Group LLC
Photography by Kris D'Amico www.krisdamico.com

Publisher's Cataloging-In-Publication Data
(Prepared by The Donohue Group, Inc.)
Webb, Chitoka.
  Something inside of me : how to hang onto heaven when you're going through hell / Chitoka Webb. — 1st ed.
  p. ; cm.
  ISBN: 978-1-934572-86-3
  1. Webb, Chitoka. 2. Self-actualization (Psychology) 3. Businesswomen—United States—Biography. 4. Young women—United States—Biography. 5. Success in business. 6. Conduct of life. I. Title.
BF637.S4 W42 2011
158.1/092   2011923949

Part of the Tree Neutral® program, which offsets the number of trees consumed in the production and printing of this book by taking proactive steps, such as planting trees in direct proportion to the number of trees used: www.treeneutral.com

TreeNeutral

Printed in the United States of America on acid-free paper

11 12 13 14 15 16   10 9 8 7 6 5 4 3 2 1

First Edition

CONTENTS

Introduction

Life is not perfect. We all make mistakes and encounter problems. In *Something Inside of Me*, I share the details of how I turned my mistakes and obstacles into miracles.

After suffering heart-wrenching experiences such as growing up in poverty, not graduating with my high school class, and being diagnosed with a debilitating disease, I discovered as I triumphed over each trial that there was one thing that was constant, true, and loving—there was something inside of me.

You may receive a hit so hard that it knocks you off your feet. My book offers you the inspiration and strength to get back on your feet and move forward with more direction and enthusiasm than before. I present the tools and lessons needed to remove the barriers that are blocking your path to fulfillment and success in life. I help you tap into something inside of you to help you triumph over the challenges you encounter.

My message is universal. We all hurt. We all cry. We must learn that if we can make it once, we can make it twice; if we can overcome disappointment once, we can overcome it twice. Holding on to heaven when we are going through hell can empower us to recover because of something inside of me and something inside of you.

1
THE WISDOM OF GROWING UP

*"The day the child realizes that all adults are imperfect, he becomes
an adolescent; the day he forgives them, he becomes an adult;
the day he forgives himself, he becomes wise."*
—Alden Nowlan

Most of the lessons I learned in life were birthed during my early
years growing up in the Preston Taylor housing projects located on
the west side of Nashville on Clifton Avenue. Preston Taylor was one
of Nashville's most powerful black leaders in the early 1900s. He
was a businessman, an undertaker, and an influential minister. The
projects were named in his honor due to countless acts of kindness
and the numerous contributions that he made to the community
throughout his life. I lived there from 1974 to late 1980. While the
community was riddled with crime and low-income families, you
could always find the spirit of sharing: either someone was knocking
on your door to borrow a cup of sugar or you were knocking on their
door to return the favor.

"Hi Mrs. Helen," I said, looking up toward the sky. Mrs. Helen was a large woman standing at six feet tall; she was also a woman with a big heart. "Hey baby, where your momma?" she said, leaning down and smiling at me. "She's washing my sister's hair, we got to go back to church," I said, my hands now slippery from twirling my hair around my fingers. My hair was freshly pressed and I could not resist. "Well, tell your momma I said thank you for letting me use her phone last night. I baked y'all a cake this morning." Everybody loved Mrs. Helen's cakes. "Now take it in there and set it on the kitchen table, and leave the wrapping on it. That'll keep it fresh," she said as she passed the cake off to me. As I walked to the kitchen the smell of warm flour and Coca-Cola sure made it tempting to lift the wrapping and lick the chocolate icing stuck to the paper. Rising early to the sweet smell of fried bacon and eggs and the thumping sound of gospel music was a ritual. When I woke up, my first taste of joy was seeing my mother's face: a twenty-seven-year-old, brown-skinned woman with a medium frame and a beautiful smile.

"Did you thank God for allowing you to see another day?" my mother asked as she shook the skillet to make sure the fried eggs didn't stick.

"Yes, maim," eased out of my mouth as I yawned last night away.

The cool aluminum dining table felt like a breath of fresh air on my warm face as I folded my arms and rested my head.

"Toke, why are you squirming around in the chair?" she said as the timer on the toaster buzzed.

"Momma, the plastic on the seat is torn and it's scraping my butt." Since I was only four years old, it never dawned on me that I could move to another chair.

"Why don't you sit in the good one?" She followed this with a wink to let me know that as bad as I thought it was, everything was okay.

My mother always made us feel like earth had no sorrows that heaven couldn't heal. She had a quote for every situation, including "Every day you wake up, you got another chance." All were her way of saying that things are never as bad as you think they are. She taught me and my two sisters early on how to make do with what we had when things ran low toward the end of the month. With her wisdom we became experts at supplementing what we had. On occasions when there was not enough money for orange juice, my sisters and I would put sugar in water. We definitely knew the difference. The orange juice was nice and smooth, especially when chilled, but sugar doesn't dissolve well in cold water no matter how much you stir. There was always the residue of small chips of sugar floating around in the glass. After each sip of this juice substitute, I could feel loads of sugar slowly dissolving on the back of my tongue. Oh! We were young, but we learned early on how to make a way out of no way.

We would douse our toast with government-issued peanut butter that came in a shiny silver can. The heck with complaining about not having grape jelly. This substitution regime was not only for food; it included games as well. No checker and monopoly games— no worries we thought. Get a piece of chalk and draw hopscotch squares on the ground. Every item in our house was made for more than one use. The dish rag would serve as a flyswatter when the flies didn't get the message that they were not welcome. Having to live with the little brown cockroaches was enough! The milk jug had nine lives: Once the milk was gone, it became the Kool-Aid jug, water jug, or a jug for any liquid concoction we came up with. If there wasn't enough money for Barbie dolls, we would dress up in our mother's clothes. We did not discriminate. If we wanted an afro, we would slap on a jerry curl bag while listening to the healing sound of Marvin Gaye. We understood that what we could not have in real life we could have in our imagination. If we wanted the long-hair look, we would slap on a pillow case and slide across the floor to the raspy sound of Diana Ross's "Ain't No Mountain High Enough." At that time, it was every little black girl's fantasy to have long hair and different colored eyes—any color but black or dark brown.

Even though we were poor, we did not know it because there was always a backup plan. It was as if everyone in the projects was born with a genius gene. It seemed embedded in our minds. But now I realize it wasn't embedded—it was taught. It was all passed down from one generation to the next. Most of these archived lessons originated from poor relatives or other people. Each generation tutored the other. There were certain things in our house that were not to be touched. For instance, if a couch had plastic on it that meant don't sit on it! Just look at it, but don't touch it. However, when we went to my aunt's house, she had two couches: the one you could sit on and the one that had plastic on it. At my grandmother's house, she had an entire living room suite that was smothered in plastic a quarter-inch thick.

I was the kid with all the questions, never fascinated with toys but mesmerized by curiosity. You know kids being kids, there was always one who would test the waters, as they say. Yep, that was me. I needed to know what the big deal was with all this plastic. On Sundays, after church, you could find Aunt Ann in the kitchen whipping up the best fried chicken in town. This was my chance to get to the bottom of plastic land. I quietly took my shoes off, stood against the wall, rocked my feet back and forth to warm them up a bit and said a prayer. I ran toward the couch like a kid being chased by a dog and dived on to the couch. Before I could get up and put on my "I-don't-know-what-happened" face, I could hear the speedy sound of shoes flapping toward me.

"You better get yo' black ass off my couch. That ain't made for you to sit on," my aunt said to me as she ran from the kitchen, with her cigarette dangling from her mouth. Well, I got my answer. After all the wondering, I learned it was just plastic.

Growing up in the projects is where I learned to let bygones be bygones. Play yard fights was how I learned to get mad as hell and get over it in the same day. I had seen more kids getting ready to fight than kids actually fighting. One day while horsing around on our homemade basketball court, ten feet of concrete with a milk crate tied to the top of a tree, two boys became angry with each other. Within seconds they had locked shoulders as the other kids circled around them moaning "whooo" before anything had even happened. Then the two boys began to repeat each other and didn't even know it.

"I ain't sc'ed of you."

"I ain't sc'ed of you," the other boy said. By now they're going around in circles, their shoulders still locked.

"Yo' mammy."

"Yo' mammy."

"That's why y'all on welfare."

"That's why y'all on welfare."

"That's what I thought."

"That's what I thought."

And without wasting another second they went back to playing basketball. By the end of the afternoon, they were swapping their Now-and-Laters and Lemon Head candies.

While we had our own way of doing things, I still had more questions bouncing around in my head: I needed to know why the men hanging out on the corners broke glass in the streets. For what? Why? There were other things that led to the list of questions in my head. I remember going to school, looking up at the bright light bulbs, and being puzzled. "Those must be the expensive ones," I thought to myself as I tried to figure out the difference between the school's bulbs and ours at home, which were a dim yellowish color. When trying to figure out the true color of a shirt, I would have to rely on the light coming in through the window. Maybe that's why, now as an adult, an old, dim light bulb makes me think back to those days of living in the projects.

Older men standing on the street corners would set the trash dumpster on fire. You always knew when they did it because the smoke would simmer its way into the house and bottles with flammable liquids and other burnable objects kept exploding. "Yep, they done set the dumpster on fire again." Hearing the sound of sirens was as normal as hearing Christmas carols in December. The sirens frightened me. Even though I knew they were not coming to my house, I would get out of bed and go cuddle with my mother. The police and firefighters looked like giant men dressed in dark clothes who made a lot of noise; at least this is what it looked like to a little girl. Either the firefighters were coming to put out the dumpster fires, or the paramedics were coming because someone got shot over a dice game. Usually it was the local police.

Either the police were raiding someone's home or chasing someone. Although they were equipped with batons and guns, they were no match for a black man running for his life. About an hour after the chase, I would see them walking back to their squad cars with no suspect in hand, wiping the sweat dripping down their necks and gasping for air. Their cheeks were red and their lips vibrated with each exhale. You could see the embarrassment on their faces, and the smiles on the faces of the women who stood in the doorways, their heads pressed against the window pane. They'd prayed to the good Lord that the police didn't catch'em and kill'em.

Prayer was something that was talked about as well as practiced. You knew these women were praying when you saw them rocking in a chair with their eyes closed and a soft grin resting across their faces. They were the ones who taught the basics to their children and the rest of the kids in the projects. I also know that these ladies are usually forgotten and never mentioned. I want to mention them because they taught me before school; they taught me before church; they taught many people's children before those kids went to Harvard. They were the cooks and nannies before we moved into this generation where successful men not only want a five-star chick, but they also want a five-star nanny. They were the ones cleaning up loose bowels packed with last night's dinner. They were always giving more than receiving. The burning smell from the stench didn't prevent them from lifting their hands toward the sky, the highest praise of appreciation. Instead of complaining about the job, they spent their time more wisely by being thankful for it, all the while gently holding others' children as if they were their own. At the same time, they silently prayed for the well-being of their children while enduring the pain of not seeing them for days at a time. They didn't have the luxury of working five days a week. They had to work all seven just to scrape up enough money to pay the rent.

They were considered just a cook, just a babysitter. But I saw something different: something on the inside kept them from losing their minds. One thing I rarely see is the examination of these women's strength. These women, and the ones long before them, had an inner strength that is unexplainable. As I grew up, I became more amazed at their ability to love during some of the most difficult times in life. For instance, there's Biddy Mason, a slave born back in the 1800s. Mason was given to her slave masters, Robert and Rebecca Smith, as a wedding present. She spent thirty-eight years in bondage. Not only was she in bondage, but so were her three daughters,

Elliott, Harriett, and Ann. All were believed to be fathered by Smith. I am sure every time she washed his smell off her, something tore within as the soul does when you are dehumanized. To spend every day on your knees cleaning, on your feet cooking, on your behind rocking babies, and then end the day on your back with the man you were given to as a wedding present is horrific and unimaginable to say the least. Years later, Mason was awarded her freedom by California judge Benjamin Hayes. Mason soon became one of the richest African-Americans in Los Angeles. She was a nurse, a midwife, a California real estate entrepreneur, and a philanthropist.

She was instrumental in founding a traveler's aid center and an elementary school for black children, and was a founding member of the First African Methodist Episcopal Church, the city's first and oldest black church. She was also one of the first African-Americans to purchase land in Los Angeles. As a businesswoman, she amassed a small fortune of nearly $300,000, which she shared generously with charities and the poor. That's a long way from the $2.50 she earned per day as a slave. She also donated money and land to schools, daycare centers, grocery stores, and churches. She regularly visited patients in nursing homes and inmates in prisons.

Mason's life is an elegant example of what life looks like when you let bygones be bygones. She made the choice to love, give love, and share love by any means necessary. There is no record of her spewing hate or blaming others for her brutal beginnings, just triumph after triumph. She is famous for the following quote: "If you hold your hand closed, nothing good can come in. The open hand is blessed for it gives in abundance even as it receives."

There is a wisdom that's vital to growing up. It is the thread I always revert to when life seems unbearable. It serves as a reminder that even though we ran low, we never ran out. Although we did not have a mansion, we had a home. We appreciated everything inside of it, from the homemade flyswatters to the mayonnaise and ketchup sandwiches, because love was something that was embedded in each of us.

2

THE LONELINESS OF BEING DIFFERENT

"There is no greater agony than bearing an untold story inside of you."
—Maya Angelou

I knew early on that I was different, but at the time I thought it was a bad kind of different. As a child, I concluded this because of the relentless negative comments some of my family, friends, and strangers made about me. I was convinced there was a sticker on my forehead that said, "Hey, over here, let me have it."

My earliest memory of feeling the pain of being different was in grade school. It started simply because I pronounced a word correctly. During the review of our words before the weekly spelling test, the teacher called on me to say the word "then."

"Chitoka," my teacher said with a mouth full of confidence, "pronounce the word that I spell: t-h-e-n."

I was home free because my mother had studied the words with me the night before. "Then," I said with a smile on my face.

"Correct, Chitoka," my teacher said. "It sounds like someone has been practicing."

I was really smiling now. I loved when one of my teachers appreciated my effort. Almost immediately my excitement was sucked away by the sound of the lunch bell ringing. We got in a straight line, which was required when we were walking to the cafeteria. The walk down the hallway was always a big to-do to us youngins. As we lined up, the girls behind me were snickering. I turned around hoping to join in on the fun; unfortunately they were laughing at me.

"You talk like a white girl," one girl said mockingly. Without hesitation, the other girl chimed in, "You're weird."

Confused by their ridiculous assessment, I asked, "Why do you think I talk like a white girl?"

The one who accused me of being weird said, "You're just different. It's the way you say stuff."

As young as I was, I knew what they were doing to me was wrong, but I was afraid to say anything because I wanted to be friends with them. But they kept on teasing me, and when we got to the cafeteria, the girl who had started the madness accused me of eating like a white person because I chose an apple over a bag of chips.

When we sat at the table, she continued to tease me: "Who taught you how to talk like that anyway?"

By then I had had enough. "My momma taught me how to talk like that—or would it help you if I said my mammie?"

Every mouth at the table dropped. The silence in the air was as thick as the bread lying on our plates. I was glad to shut them up long enough to eat my lunch. My walk home that day was a lonely one—the first of many. I didn't know it then, but I learned an important lesson that day: People who have a problem with you being different actually have a problem with themselves. As I got older, I realized that these people did not have a problem with me personally. They really had a deep-seated hatred or fear of that which threatens them because it is different. When I got home I slammed my books down on the table as the oppressive emotions ran through my body. I wanted to be so mad at them that I could not possibly ever see being friends with them again, but I couldn't. Even though the teasing caused my heart to feel like it had been cooked, I could not convince myself to dislike them.

A few years later, I learned another lesson the hard way. I befriended a white girl who had moved into our apartment complex during the summer. We developed a good relationship and would talk on the phone for hours. I felt like I had finally found a friend who I could trust. It would be short-lived.

On a hot Saturday evening we were outside playing with our Cabbage Patch dolls. She had a white one and I had a black one. So for fun we switched. While I was playing with her doll and admiring its smile, I was suddenly distracted by the sound of someone briskly running up a hill. I put my hand in front of my eyes to keep the sun from blinding me and looked up at the top of the hill. My friend was waving my doll around by the hair and saying, "Chitoka, look at the nigger baby." I almost fell over on my face because she had never said anything like that before. I considered her to be my best friend because she always told me how pretty I was.

As I snuggled in bed that night, I remember feeling angry and wondering why I couldn't get it right. I felt like I was a magnet for brutality and told myself that it hurts being me. It seemed as if my sheer presence was a disappointment and that no matter where I went this reality would follow me. When I went to church I was mocked by the greeter with the bad feet and would always steel myself against what felt like bullets when she spoke.

"What you smiling about now?" the greeter would ask. "Every time I see you, you smilin'."

I was always confused because she never asked the little girl before me why she was always frowning or complaining. I would have to endure this type of ridicule every other day. "You sho' is a pretty little girl to be so black," the drunk uncle at the family reunion would remind me when I arrived. He would then look at my older sister, who is light-skinned and say, "Gul you still pretty." I searched high and low trying to find out what the problem was, why was I so different. Even being quiet couldn't save me, and neither could smiling. I always managed to find myself on the other side of the stick. My oldest sister and I are four years apart, but ever since I can remember we have always been the same size. To stretch out the few outfits we had, we would share clothes. The problem was, she never wanted to share her clothes with me. Her constant rejection diminished the crust of my confidence.

My mother was in the kitchen one Sunday afternoon preparing dinner. The steam from the fat meat and the turnip greens had settled into the walls. I noticed when I slightly leaned my head as I tried to connect with my mother's eyes. "Momma," I said with my bottom lip hanging low. "Yes , baby?" She was looking at me and stirring at the same time, and she could see that I was upset.

"Momma, I let Trisha wear all the clothes in my closet, and when I asked her if I could wear her pants, the white ones with the squirrelly paint marks, she told me no." As she took the butter knife and made a clean incision down the middle of the cornbread, she glanced at my reaction. My skin was no longer smooth like melted chocolate but full of wrinkles that looked like shady rows of packed skin. "Well, next time you tell her no" she said, then swung the kitchen towel over her shoulders, letting me know that's how you solve that. A bit of confusion began to circumvent inside of my mind. "I can't" dribbled out of my mouth slowly. "I can't tell her no."

The smell of Palmolive dishwashing liquid made my nose crinkle as my mother grabbed my face. "And why not," she said, holding my small face in her hand.

"I don't know how," I said with my eyes moving from side to side.

"Well that may be something you need to pray about."

I went to my room, got down on my knees, and closed my eyes so tight, hoping to trap the tears. "Dear God, I don't want to be like this anymore, make me mean." I took a deep breath because the tears had seeped into my mouth. I kept praying. "God, something is wrong with me and everybody knows it but me. Make me mean." At the time I knew God could do anything, but I did not know that asking God to make me different than how he made me was the same as telling God that he'd made a mistake. Hours later my sister barged into the room as I was sobering up. She asked if she could wear my Al B. Sure! T-shirt and without hesitating I said yes. If sealing the deal with meanness required me to be selfish I would surely fail. Considering the alternative, I figured that I had a better chance at being happy by accepting who I was instead of praying to be some one else.

Please don't take my childhood memories as complaints. Rather they're just a reminder of what life looks like for a lot of children who are different and who have not developed the mental capacity to know that it's not a curse but a gift. Interestingly enough, when we were created, we were all created different. There are no two people in the world who have the same fingerprint. And some people are not only different, but they also posses an ability that no one else in the world could imitate.

Let's take Michael Jackson for example. Ever since I can remember there has always been someone imitating him. I admit there were some who almost had me fooled, but there was something about Michael Jackson that when you saw him, you knew it was him. Honestly, I don't know if it was the way he walked or talked, but there was something that made him stand out. And being different myself, I would soon find out that it was his spirit. His spirit was the one thing that couldn't be copied by someone else. The spirit is the core of the soul. There is nothing behind the core of your soul but the hand of the creator, just like there is nothing behind the birth of a newborn but the womb of a woman. The core is the root of who you are in its truest form: It is only capable of functioning as is. The spirit is a fundamental emotional principle that determines one's character. In other words, no matter how much you dress yourself up, your spirit will always shine forth. While there were many imitators, there was only one Michael Jackson.

In our society, we praise those who possess special gifts. But history reveals over and over again that people with special gifts often don't feel special during their childhood. Childhood is often the most difficult time for a person who is different because the brain is not yet mature enough to perceive a negative remark for just that, a remark. Instead children perceive it as truth. Children don't have time to figure out the meaning behind the madness. Children want to be liked. They want to fit in. They want you to like their ideas. They want you to acknowledge their new shoes. They want to be told how wonderful they are. They want to feel like they matter. The little boy wants to hear his father say, "Wow, you threw that football so far I lost sight of it." The little girl wants her mother to say, "I'm glad you're my daughter." An eight-year-old girl does not understand why the girl who wears a size ten in women's shoes picks on her because she wears a size seven in girl's shoes. That little girl begins to think that her feet are too tiny, not realizing that the other girl feels bad because she thinks her own feet are too big. So she begins to beat herself up for something that she will be grateful for when she's older—having normal size feet. She's just too young to understand the grim reality of jealousy.

I cannot say that as you get older it gets better, but it does get easier. Age gives you the ability to see over mountains, and when you can see over them, your soul exhales as your hearts sighs: "And this too shall pass." Even when the pain feels like a living hell, age teaches you that though pain runs deep, it also runs out. Try crying your heart out when it has been broken, and you'll see that as you release the pain, you'll eventually forget what you were crying about. I have learned from being different that pain is part of the package, and after a while—as odd as this may sound— you will learn to appreciate it for what it is worth.

I believe that "no" is the gift that nobody wants, and pain is the gift that nobody understands. For example, when I was a child my mother loved to go to garage sales. It was a Saturday ritual for her. The challenge for me was I did not like to go: The idea of getting in and out of a car every other block was of no interest to my ten-year-old self. Daydreaming about all the things that little girls imagine at ten seemed sweeter to me than rummaging through old clothes and stained pillows that smelled like they had been soaked in hot sweat. Since my mother always managed to find a parking space in front of the house where the sale was taking place, she was able to shop freely while I stayed in the car to talk to my imaginary friends who lived in the back window.

This Saturday was extremely hot outside. I wasn't bothered by it because no one in my neighborhood had an air conditioner in their car, so I was used to the heat. With the windows down, the hot air filled the car. As I talked to my imaginary friends and looked out the back window, I heard this buzzing sound, but I did not see a bee. *Buzz. Buzz. Buzz.* Then I happened to look down at my folded arms resting at the edge of the back seat. A bee was caught in the crease that connected the headrest and the liner of the back window. I looked at it, amazed at how big the belly was. Then I looked at its black, shiny eyes. I was so close I could see its legs vibrating and knew it was stuck. So I decided to pull the bee out, not to save it, but to kill it.

So I picked the bee up and after five seconds I knew I did not like it. I remember looking at the bee and thinking, *I am going to squeeze the life out of you.* My mind was made up. I began to squeeze the bee. A warm secretion squirted onto my fingernail and then my finger felt like it was on fire. The pain was so intense I threw my head back and took a deep breath. By now the bee was lying lifeless in the back window, and my index finger had a pin drop of blood seeping through this tiny hole. Now I really didn't like the bee, but the pain forced me to think past my dislike. I sat there staring at the dead bee, thinking, *You stung me!* Then my young mind said, *But you started all of this. The bee was reacting to your action. Your dislike for the bee got the better of you, and you thought you had the right to kill it.* Whew! The pain had spread through my entire hand, and I thought about why I took advantage of the bee being helpless. Why did I smile knowing that I was the only person who could save the bee?

Pain forces you to do something different the second time around. Pain helps you understand that there is more to the situation than your own feelings. It is our familiarity with pain that keeps us from hurting others. I've never killed another bee, and when I see one now, I think about the one that I hurt for no reason twenty-five years ago. Not only is pain a gift, so is being different. You need both to become the brilliant person you were designed to be.

3

THE GOOD THING ABOUT STRUGGLING

"Where there is no struggle, there is no strength."
—Oprah Winfrey

As I said before, "no" is the gift that nobody wants. The older I get, the more I believe that this is true. But I had to learn this lesson the hard way during my senior year of high school.

A week before my high school graduation in 1993, I was headed to class when my guidance counselor, Mrs. Covington, called me into her office. When I approached the office, I was more curious than concerned. I had just finished practicing for the graduation ceremony; my senior pictures had been taken; and I had mailed more than fifty invitations to family members and friends. So for the next week, I was just going through the motions. Oh, I was just cruising! As far as I was concerned, my diploma already had my name on it.

The padded chair in the counselor's office hissed as I plopped into it.

"Chitoka, you're not going to graduate," Mrs. Covington said, not wasting any time getting to the point.

I stared at her, not fully comprehending her words.

"I'm not going to graduate?" I finally managed to croak as my head began to spin.

After years of hard work, suddenly my dream of graduating from high school was being snatched away. My stomach churned into knots and my mouth felt sticky. As I took a hard swallow the inside of my jaws stuck to my teeth—my nerves had made the saliva resting in my mouth gooey. Mrs. Covington had more pictures on her wall than an art museum. I focused on one, hoping that the painting would pull me from my place of despair. I tried to find a way to rewind my life back a few minutes so I could regroup, but there were no buttons to push, no possible way to step back into the reality before I walked into the room. It was gone forever.

"Why not?" I asked softly. "Are you sure you have the right person?"

Mrs. Covington glanced at a piece of paper, which I assumed was my grades. Then she looked at me. "You are Chitoka L. Webb, aren't you?" she asked sarcastically.

I gave a hesitant nod as though I were hearing my name for the first time.

"You don't have enough credits to graduate. You need twenty-two, but you only have twenty-one and a half."

I continued to stare at her, thinking this was a nightmare from which I would soon awake. The mental rush of disbelief made my brain freeze. *Why are you telling me this a week before graduation?* I thought. What about all the invitations I had sent out? Family and friends were coming to celebrate with me on this special day. Graduating from high school was a dream that I had worked hard for, and now the fear of being excluded from this special day made me feel nauseous. How was I going to tell my mother and the rest of my family I wasn't graduating? My mind was spinning. I was so disappointed because I had only one chance to walk with my graduating class, and if I missed that date, I would never have that chance again. How could I tell my family and friends that there was a change in plans because of something as trivial as half a credit?

"Is there anything I can do to make it up?" I finally managed to ask. Even though my brain felt like it had frost on it, to my surprise it was still working. Surely there must be something I can do, I thought.

Mrs. Covington shook her head. I thought I could see regret in her eyes—or maybe it was pity. "I'm sorry," she said. "Your chemistry grade is what's hurting you. You have a sixty-nine and you need a seventy to get the half credit you need to graduate."

I was so close to accomplishing something that was extremely important to me. The nerves in my face no longer felt like tiny cells but instead like the belly of fast-moving maggots. The anxiety was moving down my neck; the reality of not reaching my goal was alive. Not reaching my goal made my nerves crawl. As I listened to Mrs. Covington speak, a flicker of hope ignited in my heart and quickly spread like wildfire through my body. I had been worried for no reason. My chemistry teacher, Mr. Lashley, was my all-time favorite teacher. I knew there was no way he was going to prevent me from graduating, not when all that stood between me and a cap and gown was a measly point.

"Don't worry," I told the counselor confidently. "I'm going to walk across that stage and get my diploma with the rest of my classmates."

She looked at me, and I knew she wanted to believe me, but there was doubt in her eyes. At that point I had enough confidence for both of us. I gathered my things and left, silently laughing to myself that she had me all stressed out for nothing. I skipped off to my chemistry class like a kid headed to the candy store. I grinned when I saw Mr. Lashley standing at the podium grading papers.

"What are you so happy about?" he asked, smiling at me.

"Mrs. Covington had me all stressed out. She called me into her office to tell me I wasn't going to graduate because I have a sixty-nine in your class and I need a seventy to graduate. Everybody knows you're my favorite teacher and . . . "

I stood there waiting for him to finish my sentence and to give me the one point. He just stared at me like he was waiting for me to continue. I laughed, thinking he was just acting silly, which he did sometimes. I stopped short when I realized he wasn't laughing with me. The joke was on me.

"And I guess you think I'm just going to give you the point so you'll have a passing grade in my class?"

I nodded slowly.

He capped his pen and laid it down on the podium before focusing on me. "Why should I give you the point, Miss Webb?" he asked sternly.

I tried to come up with a good answer, but because you're my favorite teacher didn't seem like the right thing to say. "It's just a point," I finally said in my defense.

He nodded and gave a tight smile. "You're right. It is just a point—a point you didn't earn. If I give you a point today, you will always expect someone to give you something for nothing, and you will never learn the lesson of working hard."

"So you're not going to do it?" He didn't know it, but this news caused me to shake inside.

"No," he said, sounding a little more kind. "Trust me, you'll thank me for this later."

The pain cut deep. It was as though I had been punched so hard in the nose that I could feel it all the way through my teeth. As I turned to leave, I felt like my life was ending. I felt rejected as I walked out the door—like there were no words left in me to speak. I clearly remember the walk to my car; it was only a few feet, but it felt like a few miles. Everything to the left and right of me was black. I could see only what was in front of me. I could not comprehend how thirteen years of rising early, being obedient, and attending classes could all be dissolved in an instant because of one measly point. I was so close, yet so far away.

When I got home that afternoon, I went straight to my room; grasping the belief that I was a failure made me feel exhausted. I couldn't bear to tell my mother what had happened. I needed more time to digest the fact that it was official—I was not going to graduate from high school. There was no way I could live with my mother's disappointment. My mind was so heavy with disbelief that I wanted to lie down and sleep forever.

"How was school, Toke?" my mother finally asked over dinner. She, like most people, called me by my nickname.

I just kind of shook my head, dreading the conversation I knew was coming. I tried not to look at her. My mother had this way about her where she could immediately perceive a person's insecurities. I knew she sensed something was wrong. I also knew if I looked into her eyes, I would break down and tell her everything. I rarely kept anything from my mother, but this was one secret I was determined to keep.

"School was fine, Mom," I said. "Kinda ready for the weekend. How was work?"

"We got some new desktop computers. My goal is to have all of them programmed by Monday." I could hear the drag in her voice. This was her way of telling me I wasn't being honest.

As my mother made small talk, I learned how teenagers found

the strength to smile at their parents during some of the most difficult times in life. I had made mistakes before as a teenager, like the
time I took everything out of the refrigerator and crawled in to keep
cool because the central air in our apartment was broken. My mother
screamed at the top of her lungs when she opened the door to find
me asleep in a fetal position. I knew she was disappointed in me, but
not graduating from high school would disappoint her even more.

I smiled as a way of saying *I am sorry that I let you down. I want
to cry, but I feel like I don't have the right. I am lost because the very
person I am hurting is the person I need to hold me so I don't fall apart.
Momma, I'm sorry.*

I cleared my throat to interrupt my thoughts and think of the
best way to tell my mother there wasn't going to be a graduation the
following week, at least not for me. I wanted to say, "I'm not going
to be able to go to the graduation. I don't have the details right now."
But I glanced at my mother and then quickly glanced at my plate
and shoveled a huge bite of food into my mouth. I followed it with a
large mouthful of water so I wouldn't have to talk.

I could feel my mother's gaze burning through me like a hot iron
smoldering its way through an ironing board cover. Embarrassment
was making me crumble from the inside out. I knew that the old
saying "What is done in the dark will eventually come to light" was
so true. What I did not know was how it was all going to come out.
I knew that this black cloud would surface soon. Besides, how long
could I tiptoe around my mother? I knew that the closer it got to
the graduation date, the discussions about the details would become
more frequent.

I was so disappointed in myself that with each breath I took, I
felt the pain of it all in my heart. The guilt weighed so heavily on
me it felt like the pressure could break through concrete. This entire

experience taught me something about myself that I will never forget: I have a big heart, and when it is broken it leaves a big bruise.

Suffering to this extent over not graduating from high school also taught me that I needed to do whatever possible to protect myself in the future. Anything that has the power to hurt me to the point that I want to give up on everything in life should be closely examined before making decisions that only added fuel to the fire. I made a commitment to myself from that day forward that I would face my troubles head on. While dodging this situation brought some measure of relief, it was only for a moment.

I also came to the realization that the storms of life will run their full course and eventually pass. With that being my foundation, I had to think of my next step. I was determined to let this one moment in time run its full course. In other words, I would cry if I needed to, mope around if I needed to, devote more time to myself if I needed to. I would just let nature take its course. Now I was on to something. At the age of eighteen, this gave me the glimmer of hope that I needed to pull myself through the guilt and shame of not graduating. I could not fathom any way that this experience could ever lead to anything good in life. Unfortunately, at eighteen you are not old enough to know that you don't know everything.

My next step was to decide how I would break the news to my family and friends. After giving it much thought, I was certain I did not have the energy or the heart to tell them. So I did not say a word to anyone. Eventually the shame mixed with the guilt made me feel selfish. My own interest or happiness took priority over everything else. My family and friends were so excited about the upcoming graduation, and I received lots of congratulatory phone calls the morning of the ceremony.

"Hey, Toke, just calling to congratulate you on your big day. I am so proud of you," my best friend said. There was one call after another— from well-wishers cheering me on.

"I will see you tonight," my mother said while clutching her keys as she prepared to leave for work. Through a light chuckle she reminded me of how proud she was as she wrapped her arms around me. Her quick kiss on the cheek left the scent of her perfume on my shirt. She was being playful.

When the day wound down, my house became extremely quiet. After six o'clock that evening, I was the only person at home. I sat in the living room watching some boring television show and the clock. Each second increased my feeling of defeat. I remembered from graduation practice that I was scheduled to walk across the stage at 7:15 p.m. At that moment I closed my eyes and said to myself, "Toke, I'm sorry for taking us through this. I will not as long as I live forget that the race is not over until you cross the finish line." The tears pushed their way through my sagging eyelids. I then silently apologized to the people who supported me by taking the time to attend my graduation. The graduation ceremony was to end around 9:00 p.m. My phone started ringing at 8:59 p.m.

"Toke, what happened to you?" my mother asked frantically. "We didn't hear your name called or see you walk across the stage."

"Mom, I'll explain everything when you get home. Where are you? On a pay phone?"

I received tons of phone calls. "Girl, what is going on?" asked one friend who had an idea of what might have happened.

I thought long and hard about sharing with them the real reason I was not at the graduation. Even though the graduation was now over, I still could not bring myself to tell them I was just one grade point shy of walking across that stage. My family knew that I had gotten a speeding ticket a month before graduation. So I had what I thought was a decent lie. I would tell them I wasn't at my graduation because I had to go to traffic school that night. I prepared myself a light snack so I could eat instead of talking, hoping this would deter my mother from letting loose on me.

When she arrived home, I told her my lie. "What? A speeding ticket?" she said. "You had to go to traffic school at seven o'clock on a Friday night?"

I nodded and shoved another forkful of food into my mouth, hoping she wouldn't expect me to talk if my mouth was full. Although I knew she didn't believe me, my mother let it go, and I breathed a sigh of relief.

That night I lay in bed praying, not that I could have graduated, although that did cross my mind, but that I would gain wisdom and understanding from this situation. I knew in the depths of my soul that I never wanted to be in a situation where I had to ask someone for something that I was responsible for earning, even something as small as a point to pass a class.

At that moment, a presence I couldn't explain arose in me, and I felt it deep down in my bones. It wasn't the first time I had felt it. It had appeared years before when I was being molested by a fifty-year-old man who lived in our apartment complex. Every time he would stand over me, his shadow completely covering my small body, something would kick in, consoling me and reminding me that I was beautiful and that wherever I wanted to go in my mind, I had a friend. Despite the devastation of that dark moment, in my life, something inside of me told me it would be over soon. In spite of what was happening to me at that very moment I was still a winner. I was determined not to let being molested make me feel like I was less.

One morning I awoke to the thought of, *Yeah, you didn't graduate, but that does not mean you will never graduate. Try again, press for-ward. Don't let this situation make you feel like you're a failure—you can change the outcome by getting the one point.* I thumbed through the phone book trying to find a summer school program that I could enroll in but they were all filled. I called my mother at work, frustrated by my unsuccessful attempts.

"Momma, I can't find anything. I have been calling everywhere," I told her. "Some schools I even called twice accidently."

Although my mother was stern and demanded respect as the head of the household, she was never forceful. I did not tell her until my mid-twenties why I did not graduate . She was always more concerned with helping me get through a situation than bashing me for making a mistake.

"I'll take my lunch break around eleven o'clock, and I'll swing by and take you to Cohn Adult Learning Center," she said. "They have classes all year round."

Her helpful tone reminded me that she was still proud of me and that even though she did not yet know why I had not graduated her feelings for me had not changed.

After all, she is the one who taught me that things are never as bad as you think they are. In May 1994, after attending summer school, I earned the half credit I needed to receive my high school diploma. I was extremely grateful for a second chance. Once again, I invited family and friends to my graduation. I also invited one special guest, Mr. Lashley, my high school chemistry teacher. While I was preparing myself for graduation that evening, I felt so happy. I learned that even if you see no end in sight, you must find the courage to hope when you think there is no hope. I can assure you that there is a ray of hope in the midst of your darkness.

When I arrived at the ceremony, my heart was warmed when I saw that Mr. Lashley was my first guest to arrive. Everything around me seemed to be shining as though the universe was smiling down on me. One thought resonated through my mind that day: *I am glad to be me.*

When I walked across the stage, I spotted my mother in the audience, and I saw tears rolling down her cheeks. The cheers of my guests were strong enough to make me feel confident about never giving up. Seeing Mr. Lashley throw me a thumbs-up as I walked to the end of the stage gave me the closure I needed.

Before Mr. Lashley left the parking lot, he looked at me with a caring smile and asked in a deep voice, "Ms. Webb, doesn't it feel better when you earn it?"

4

MOVING ON

"Success is not final, failure is not fatal:
it is the courage to continue that counts."
—*Winston Churchill*

By 1999, I had found my niche. Not only had I finished barber
school, but I had become a master barber. Only a few women in
Nashville had the distinction of being able to perform all the duties
of a barber, including using a straight-edged razor for shaves and
haircuts and being able to dye hair and beards. It was evident that
I had a gift. For most the evidence was the immaculate haircuts. I
knew my talent was special because of the feelings in my hand, and
my ability to visualize my clients' completed haircuts before they
even walked in the door. Then somehow this information would be
communicated to my hands and before long my eyes could only see
the best haircut possible. Over the years while barbering, I learned
that when a client is in need of a good haircut, they should start by

locating a barber with a good attitude because the frame of mind is going to come out in the haircut.

Being a barber was not something that I thought about growing up. As a matter of fact, I don't even know if I had ever mentioned the word "barber" when I was young. One day while taking a nap on a Saturday afternoon, I was awakened by a strange feeling in my hands. I really didn't think much of it. It wasn't painful at all. It felt more like anxiety. Later that day, my boyfriend of three weeks and I were sitting on my patio talking about nothing when I came up with the bright idea of cutting his hair. Of course, he was reluctant. Most teenage boys would not be enthusiastic about a eighteen-year-old girl cutting their hair for the first time.

"You don't know how to cut hair," he said as a hard frown broke across his face.

"Yes, I do. I can feel it in my hands," I said, trying to persuade him.

He then blurted out, "You never told me that."

"I know. I just found out myself," I said, looking at him with my eyes bulging. Come on. Let me try."

He dropped his head in his hands and said, "Girl, if you mess me up . . . "

Excited by his approval, I jumped up and said, "Boy, be quiet. I am not going to mess you up."

At least in my mind I believed I was not going to mess him up. I liked him so I definitely did not want to do anything to make him angry. But the massacre began.

"I want it bald on the sides, faded in and lined up in the front," he said in a trembling voice. Over the years, I have learned that men are just as self-conscious about their hair as women.

"Okay, now I need you to be real still," I said with a heap of confidence. The power button on the clippers was still in the off position.

I was well on my way. I had skinned the sides. They were as smooth as a newborn baby's bottom. Then I gently smoothed out the top. The last step was to fade in the top with the sides so that it would not look like a bowl cut. I knew that was one haircut boys did not want to be caught dead with. When it was time to fade in the sides, I panicked. I had never seen a barber blend in a haircut before. I could feel the knot in my throat slide down into my gut.

"What's taking you so long? Don't you feel it in your hands?" he teased as if the joke was on me.

"I am trying . . . Okay, I don't think I am going to be able to finish," I said abruptly. "I can't blend it in." I smacked my lips to finish my sentence as if it was no big deal.

As he huffed and puffed, his reasons for being outraged became clear to me. This was a Saturday evening, and the barbershops were closed and would not reopen until Tuesday. I could see the regret in his eyes. He would never forgive himself for allowing me to screw up his hair. After he left, I went to my room and felt down because he had to wear that bowl cut for three more days to church, to work, and in the community. Needless to say he broke up with me, and I never heard from him again. I learned that night that sometimes natural talent requires training and guidance to develop.

Fortunately, my barbering career had a much better ending. After I received my master barber license in 1999, I learned that the key to success was the ability to listen to the customer. When customers could not translate their wishes into words, I was responsible for helping them flesh out the image they saw in their mind. The first and only barbershop in Nashville that I had the privilege of working in was Tonya's Barbershop on Joe Johnston Avenue. A few weeks after earning my barber license, I received a phone call from a woman who had the voice of someone who could be trusted.

"May I speak with Toke please?" she asked in a dainty voice as I was leaving my house in search of work.

"This is she," I said in a confused tone because I did not recognize her voice.

"I have heard a lot about you," she said. "I would love to meet and talk with you about working in my barbershop."

I smiled so big that my lips could feel the tiny holes in the phone receiver. "Sure, when would you like to meet?" I said as I stood in the doorway hoping that she would say today.

"I have some time around noon today. Will that work for you?"

"You bet," I said, not giving it a second thought. "I will see you at noon." I was delighted that my search ended as quickly as it had begun.

When I walked in, the glass-covered window shades and the electric barber chairs made me feel like I was in a museum. This was the most beautiful barbershop that I had ever seen in my life: I was even more amazed to see the faces of people that I had seen only on television.

"Hi my name is Toke," I said as the door automatically locked behind me.

"Hey, girl, I am glad you came," she said. Her customer peeked through the hot towel wrapped around his head. He tried to get a glimpse of my face as he spoke in a hushed manner. "Tonya is that girl they said cuts hair real good?"

I didn't know that I was already well known within the barbering community. Before we even began our conversation, I had made up my mind that I wanted to work there. Now all I needed to know was when I could start. I had put my clippers in the trunk just in case the meeting was a success.

I remember the first few weeks being slow, not for Tonya, but for me. She had appointments every thirty minutes. During my time working there I rarely saw her sit down. She made using a straight-edged razor look as easy as writing with a pencil. I watched her every move because I didn't want to let her down. I caught on quickly, and soon my appointment book was filled from the time we opened until the time we closed. And the money was rolling in. I went from making about $300 a week after paying the rent for my booth to $800 a week within a month.

The money was good, and it brought out my lack of business sense. I spent money on random things, and I was always hustling at work to make enough money by 10 a.m. to pay the electric bill before the lineman came to disconnect my service. While the work was steady and things appeared to be going well, my personal life was spinning out of control. Now when I look back, I realize that most of my actions were done out of pure ignorance. I didn't have the backbone to say "no" to my elders who kept asking me for money so they could buy things that they said they needed. I had not learned that saying "no" was not a crime and that God was not going to be angry with me for using my money for what I needed.

I also started smoking Black and Mild cigars, which a guy I had dated introduced me to. As time went on, the cigars seemed to taste better when smoked with a glass of brandy. This combination enhanced my taste for something stronger. Eventually, I was smoking cigarettes and marijuana and drinking alcohol almost daily. Strangely, the more marijuana I smoked, the more I wanted to listen to gospel music. One day while smoking a joint as thick as an Oscar Mayer hot dog with my cousin Bam, I stuck in a gospel CD and turned the volume up.

"Girl, what's wrong with you? Now ain't the time to be listening to that."

The seeds in the joint popped from my hard draw. "Just listen to the words," I said as a woman belted out, "Can't nobody do me like Jesus." It was evident that I was blowing his high.

"You know I used to tell my mother when I was younger that you were weird, but now I realize it's even deeper than that," he said and then swallowed the last of his powered doughnuts.

I tried to maintain my position as a functioning druggie, but I was losing my grip. My life was headed off the cliff. I could hear the sound of dusty rocks crumbling under my feet. When they fall and you don't hear them crashing at the bottom you know you are at the end. A sound mind would turn around; a diseased mind thinks there is more room for error.

I knew I had hit rock bottom when my nights of fun started ending at six o'clock in the morning. I'd then race to the barbershop to prepare for my eight o'clock clients. Sometimes I would work for days at a time without any rest.

The situation that changed it all was an encounter with a police officer after one of my nights of fun. Around five o'clock on this particular morning, I decided to make my way to the barbershop to get ready for my first client. I was headed for a railroad crossing when I was suddenly stopped by a police officer. I was a little concerned since we were in a secluded area on the north side of town, and it was very dark outside. None of that prevented him from motioning me to stop on the railroad tracks. I thought that was a little strange. But he was the police officer and I was being pulled over, so I respected his command. Before he got to my window, I could smell the alcohol reeking off his skin. I could taste it in my mouth. His eyes were bloodshot.

"What are you doing on this side of town at this time of night?"

"Officer, I am headed to work." I could not believe it, but he asked me if I had been drinking. "No, sir," I quickly replied.

"Good, don't start. Have a good night and drive safely," he said sternly.

I was so frightened and confused by what had just happened. All I wanted was to get off those railroad tracks and get to a safe place. I began telling myself no more late night outings. Even though this situation was not tragic, I learned two things about tragedy that night: It travels to you without warning, and you travel toward it with warning and full understanding.

As bad as I wanted to change, I knew complete change would take some drastic actions on my part. How could I do it? My only draw toward confidence was a vision in my mind. I often wondered where it came from. Why did I believe so strongly in it while my friends and relatives couldn't care less about a vision lingering in one's mind? It was telling me, *Yes, you can.* It danced around in my mental space like there was no tomorrow; it was relentless. How could I get to this place I dreamed about day and night where I could live a life of peace and a life of passion? The people in my vision were kind, giving, and willing to hold you accountable, and they invited you to do the same. There was no blame. Reminders of what you are not and never will be were strictly prohibited. I envisioned people treating each other with love and respect regardless of our noticeable differences. In my vision, being human was more important than race; loving yourself and others superseded conforming to religion; and being submissive and respectful toward the creator took precedence over becoming a slave to the market's newest product. The people were polite and did you no harm. They listened more than they talked. The tune in my head got louder and louder. I lived with the constant reminder, *You can do better and you can do better now.*

But I did not know where to start, what to do first, or who to tell. So I kept quiet. I hoped that whatever this was waking up with me in the morning and going to bed with me at night would eventually give me more information. I needed to get out of the natural rhythm of mediocrity. As the stagnant routine of life played out right before my eyes, I painfully watched people around me on a road to nowhere, and I was right there with them. I believed in the highest power, and at the same time, I was living a life that reflected a big bundle of **nothing**. I had no resources, no money, and little education. And the most distressing thing was that I believed that prayer was a substitute for hard work, and that it would all get better with no action on my end. My diseased mind, the refusal to do that of which you are most capable, made me feel like I was in hell. I was sinking into a hole mentally. In my heart I knew life did not have to be this way. I would rather hoof it on to glory than to continue to live in such a raggedy mental state. I was living a life that I knew was causing my soul to rot. Eventually it got the best of me. Over and over I thought, *If I don't leave this place I am going to die.*

A crisis with my dog, Chocolate, helped pushed things along. Chocolate was a beautiful brown American cocker spaniel with big brown eyes and a white streak down the middle of his chest. He was given to me by my cousin Stacey. He treated me better than most people did. It didn't matter when I came home or what kind of mood I was in, he was always happy to see me.

"Good morning," I said to him as I got out of bed on this fateful day. He immediately came to me, eager to greet me. He nipped at my heels as I prepared for my day. I happily played with him, once again thankful to Stacey for giving me him. As I was headed out the door to work, Chocolate looked longingly outside with his big, brown puppy dog eyes.

"We'll have to wait until I come back home. Then we can go outside and play," I assured him. "I promise this evening, we will."

He whimpered as though he understood what I was saying and didn't approve.

"Chocolate," I said, "You know I have to go to work. I promise I'll take you out as soon as I get home."

He continued to stare at me. I almost relented, but I didn't want to be late for my seven o'clock appointment. I had gained a reputation for being on time and being professional, and it was something I took pride in.

"How about I leave you outside on the deck?" I asked. "It's going to be such a nice day. I know you'll enjoy it."

Chocolate jumped up, barking his approval. I laughed. I got his leash and tied him to the deck. I headed off to work, looking forward to spending time with my friend that evening when I returned. On my way to the barbershop, I thought about the many reasons why Chocolate made me happy. What came to mind almost instantly was the consistency in his affection toward me. When I arrived home, he would run toward me, jump up, and whine in an excited manner. This was not only when I was absent for a few hours, but also when I was out of his sight for a few minutes. He had me mesmerized. I am not sure if it was his affection toward me or if it was his physical appearance. He had round, light brown eyes and a shiny, wavy coat that felt like a piece of India's finest silk. What I knew for sure was that we had a bond. I was looking forward to many more years of arriving home to find Chocolate waiting for me to walk through the door.

The morning went by quickly. When my grandmother called, I was just finishing with a customer and preparing myself for my next one.

"How are you?" she asked.

"Good," I said. "We're a little busy today. Can I call you back in a little bit?"

Strange, I thought. Although my grandmother and I spoke by phone periodically, it was out of character for her to call me during the day. After giving it much thought, I considered it no big deal, so I continued to cut hair. That's when I received two more phone calls back to back—one from my mother and the other from my sister. Both asked me the same question that my grandmother had. Either they were being extremely thoughtful or something terrible had happened. Within seconds of my hanging up the phone, my cousin walked through the door of the barbershop. She motioned for me to come outside. She immediately asked me if everything was fine.

"Yes," I said, wondering why she asked. "What's going on?" I asked once we were outside, trying not to let my anxiety show.

"Toke, Chocolate's dead," she said gently.

"What?" I said. Her words just didn't make sense to me. I had just seen my dog that morning when I left him outside on the deck.

"Instead of walking down the steps, he jumped over the balcony and he hung himself," she explained.

"Oh, okay," I said, shrugging my shoulders. I immediately thought it would all be okay. *I will fix it when I get home.*

"You okay?" she asked, looking at me strangely.

It was no secret how much I loved my dog. Looking back now, I realize I was in total denial and in shock. I went back inside the barbershop like nothing had happened. But the shock was all over my face because one of the customers studied me for a moment and asked, "Are you okay?"

"I'm fine," I said, focusing on my customer. "My dog just died."

A collective "whoa" went up from the group inside the shop. I managed to tune that out as well as the condolences. I was determined to focus on my customer. When the phone rang, I sighed, not wanting to deal with another interruption. When I answered the phone, I heard my mother's voice.

"Toke, I'm going to take Chocolate to the doggie morgue. Do you want to see him before I do?" my mother asked in a soft, sad voice.

"Yes," I said, still not fully comprehending that my dog was dead.

Somehow I managed to finish with all of my customers as the reality of Chocolate's death set in. That ride home was the longest, most painful ride of my life: the thought of him hanging there all day long swinging back and forth was so agonizing that it split me open on the inside. All I could think about was getting to my friend and finding a way to fix the situation. The closer I got to my home, the more I realized that I could not fix it. My love, my friend, was gone forever. I knew it was true when I walked around to the back of the house and screamed out, "Oh, Chocolate, no!" The pain felt like hot vomit in my throat. "No, no, Chocolate, no!" For the first time my presence couldn't make him move. I was a nervous wreck. As always, my mother was supportive, but there was only so much she could do.

She had wrapped Chocolate in a white sheet. Seeing my friend lying there so still on the very picnic table that we had enjoyed together so many times before was like slicing my heart in half and pulling it apart. I apologized to him for being careless. As I sat there holding him, I realized that when it is over, it is over. And when that time comes, you better be satisfied with your actions because that is all she wrote. Losing my best friend Chocolate made me realize that life was too short. Suddenly the small tug on my heart to leave Nashville became this huge push that I couldn't ignore. It seemed I had ignored the thought for as long as I could.

That was it! I was convinced that the only way to understand the thoughts in my mind was to act on them. I knew my only hope was to move away. So I wrote down seven things I wanted to accomplish in my new city:

- To find out what was missing in my life.
- To change my mind so that I could change my unhealthy eating habits.
- To save money.
- To read as many books as I could.
- To learn to be okay with my lot in life.
- To never turn back.
- To return to Nashville and open my own barbershop.

One of my aunts lived in Atlanta, Georgia, so I contacted her, told her my plans, and asked if I could move in with her. So in 1999 I left Nashville and went to live with my aunt.

5

CHANGING LANES

"It is not the strongest of the species that survives,
nor the most intelligent that survives.
It is the one that is the most adaptable to change."
—*Charles Darwin*

So Atlanta it was. Atlanta is often referred to as "the ATL," "Hot-lanta," or "the A-town," depending on the vocabulary in your head. When I arrived, I felt like a fish out of water. Everything looked different. The streets were longer—some stretched for miles. The mist of glitz and glamour lay softly in the air. Immediately upon my arrival, I knew I had made the right decision. Realizing this caused me to look up and quietly sigh, *Thank You!* Something inside of me belted out, *Finally!*

Even though the fear of the unknown had me shaking in my boots, I was determined not to turn back until I had accomplished the things I had on my agenda. When I was in Nashville writing my plan, I decided not to put a deadline on achieving my goals. It reminded me too much of my past. I had seen dreams destroyed simply because the goal was too big for the time frame. For example, if I gave myself two weeks to lose ten pounds, by the end of the second week, if I had lost only eight pounds, I was not satisfied. I would give up without giving myself credit for the weight I had lost or the discipline I learned that could lead to better eating habits. So instead of worrying about deadlines, I focused on getting the job done. I knew I had two options: either grow up or give up. In this next stage of my life, I wanted to know what it was like to live as an adult and take responsibility for everything that came my way. I did not know where this experience would lead me, but what I did know was something inside of me felt right. The voices that had kept me up at night seemed to be resting now. Whatever this was inside of me, it was evident that it only wanted the best for me—it only had the power to push me up.

Before I moved to Atlanta, I had visited different barbershops seeking employment. Now that I had arrived, I revisited my list. I located an upscale barbershop that was owned by an older black gentleman. Besides the owner, there were two other male barbers and two female beauticians who worked there. My first visit was great. The people were polite and the owner encouraged me to come back for a second interview. I informed him that I would bring some pictures of my work. I was grateful to have found something so soon. During the next interview, I showed the owner my portfolio which I was certain would boost my chances of getting hired. Once he reviewed my photo album, he told me that he would call me during the week. I never heard from him again. Later I realized that my talent intimidated the owner.

I knew I would find the right barbershop so I kept looking.

On a breezy Thursday morning, my best friend Gwen and I were ready to hit the pavement; she had flown in the day before to join me on my search. Gwen was a fast driver; bracing myself before we went over each hump in the road was like preparing for takeoff on an airplane. The drive time from my house to downtown was a fifteen minutes, and Gwen made sure we got there in six minutes. We pulled onto Peachtree Street to find a very large group of men standing on both sides of the street, packed into the alleys that separated the tall buildings. The presence of so many bodies jammed into the pint-sized space gave off the aura of a riot. As we looked for a place to park, I felt uneasy, but Gwen was truly frightened. She looked at me with terror in her eyes. "Girl, is this the place we're looking for? What is the address on the paper?" she said as she rolled up the windows and locked all the doors. She repeatedly clicked the door locks, grabbing the attention of one of the men walking by on her side of the car. "What is he laughing at?" she squealed.

I tried to comfort her. "Gwen, honey, he's laughing at you." My tone was soft. "The doors are not going to get any more locked, so stop locking the dang doors," I said so loudly the force from my breath pushed my bangs up off of my forehead. "Okay, okay, I'm calming down," she said.

"Good. Take a deep breath because you're going to need it." She looked at me as if the situation couldn't get any worse. "This is the address were looking for and they're staring at our license plate. Don't worry, pull in right here and park."

Gwen froze. "Girl, oh no, they know we're from Tennessee! We're dead!" Her trembling voice let me know that I was going to have to think for her and for me. "Just follow me and play along," I said as we both hopped out of the car.

As predicted, a group of them began to surround us. Something inside of me knew that we had not walked into a riot but into a scam.

The man in the center was holding a square-shaped piece of torn cardboard with three gold liquor bottle tops sitting on top. I soon figured that the men walking by were also part of the scam.

"Man, I told you not to play that game!" one man shouted as he walked from the sidewalk towards the noisy group. Being surrounded so suddenly had Gwen in a frenzy. "Just do what I do," I whispered to her as she walked behind me like a scared pup.

"Well, looka here, two beautiful ladies from Tennessee," one man said. They thought they had hit the jackpot, but they were wrong. As I looked at the leader of the group I thought about one of Oprah Winfrey's quotes: "I'm easy to look at but so hard to see." His mouth moved fast like a beast with gnashing teeth and was dripping with gooey saliva as if excited by the kill. Something inside of me said, Smile and keep walking.

"If you can pick the top that has the ball up under it, I'll give you twenty dollars. If you lose, you owe me twenty dollars," the dean of flimflam said, followed by a sly giggle. I smiled and kept walking, Gwen followed, and it was evident that she had been coached. On queue, she'd smile, showing all thirty-two teeth in her mouth, and quickly snap her head in an up-and-down motion while clutching her purse. We continued to walk and smile. Pressing our way through the crowd brought some measure of relief. Once we got across the street and around the corner, I began to laugh hysterically. Looking at Gwen still smiling and shaking her head made me laugh even more. I tapped her on the shoulder. "Gwen, it's over. We made it through. You can stop acting now."

Her face relaxed. "After this, I ain't going nowhere else with you I want to go back to Nashville, tooonight," she said abruptly.

The experience was worth it. I got the job. I was hired during the first interview. Here is where my life shifted! This was one of the largest barbershops in Atlanta. There were fourteen male employees—twelve male barbers, one male beautician, and one man who shined shoes. To them I was like someone who had landed on Earth from Mars. I was the only female and I was from Nashville, Tennessee. The other barbers who were not originally from Atlanta were from Chicago, Los Angeles, New York, and other large cities. Working in the barbershop was an unforgettable experience. The conversations were interesting. And there were self-made salesmen. Whatever you wanted to buy, whether legal or illegal, there was a man who would sell it to you (e.g., herb man, glass man, oil man, shoe man, shirt man, CD man).

The beginning was somewhat challenging, but I was grateful to the owners for giving me a chance. In my short career as a barber up to that point, I was used to arriving on time and treating the customer with the utmost respect. In some ways it was different here. Across from the barbershop was Atlanta's federal building and the underground mall. It was common for a barber to leave his customer in the chair while he went across the street to the mall. Some customers waited in the chair draped and with a half haircut for hours.

The owners had decided when they opened the barbershop that they would not give anyone else a key. So I would arrive at eight o'clock in the morning and have to wait outside for hours with my clients. On one occasion, the barber scheduled to open at eight o'clock in the morning was close to four hours late. And it was raining hard. With each rain drop that trickled through my hair and landed on my eyelashes, I began to grow angry. I watched my customer struggle with hiding his watch under his sleeve. His disgust was as evident as the mist forming on the face of his watch. There was a familiar thought poking out in my mind: *Things don't have to be this way.* I felt helpless watching my customer wrestle to keep his personal belongings from being ruined by the rain. I suggested that he make his way to his next appointment. I assured him that I would contact him once I got inside of the barbershop, but he refused.

"Real men don't leave women out in the rain," he said.

I was pleased by his consideration. I started to think of ways to change the situation. Our dilemma was that we both had parked three blocks away, and none of the other businesses, including the barbershop, had an awning. While my plan was stirring in my head, out of the blue, the barber responsible for opening the shop walked right past us as if we were invisible. "Aw man, ain't nothing going on, I'm about to open the shop. Let me hit you back," he said to the person on the phone. At the root of all evil is selfishness. As he pressed the end button on his phone with the green case decorated with dollar signs, he began to flip through his keys. He did not greet us or apologize for being almost four hours late. Of the three men who owned the shop, Mel was the total jerk. He was arrogant and rude. He was the one who left his clients waiting in the chair for hours and arrived late every morning to open the barbershop. My booth rental was $175 a week, and most of the time I paid a month in advance. So when Mel arrived late to open the barbershop, it struck a nerve that I did not know I had.

Later that week we had a meeting. As Mel sat there chewing on a root stick, I could see the evil in his eyes. Looking at him took me back to one of my earliest encounters with him. One afternoon while I was eating some hot wings from a local restaurant, Mel walked up to me and started gritting his teeth together like a horse, causing his temples to push in and out. I sat there looking at him thinking, *Does this ninny think he's intimidating me?* Then he reached down and put his hands in my food and began to eat my hot wings. He never uttered an unkind word, but I could see the hate peeping from behind his pupils.

I politely pushed the hot wings toward him and said, "Looks like you need these a lot more than I do."

What I learned that day was when you have an ultimate goal you have to pick and choose your battles. If you waste your time entertaining people who are a lost cause, you will find yourself unconsciously dancing to the beat of their tune. My desire was to become the best person I could be on the inside. I had no time to entertain anyone who would keep me from reaching my goal.

Mel made a mistake. He thought I was a pushover because I was from Nashville and I was short, overweight, and dark-skinned. Unfortunately, he forgot to consider one factor: There was a strong woman in me that had been raised by another strong woman. And the women in the South don't raise no punks! Although we were poor that did not stop my mother from teaching me and my sisters principles. Her favorite was "Always treat people the way that you want to be treated." As I got older, I realized that people should in turn treat me the same way.

Mel also did not know that I was driven by an appetite for excellence. We were scheduled to have a meeting in the next two days. The way he treated everyone had gone on too long, and I was past ready to address all of the issues that concerned me, including not having a key to open the barbershop, the broken pump on my barber chair, and my station's loose countertop. When some of the large men bumped into my station, my countertop would slide to the ground, along with everything on it.

The meeting was scheduled to begin at 7:00 p.m. on Saturday night; fortunately most of us were already there. I snuck away to the bathroom, which was located in a tight space in the back of the barbershop—two small rooms conjoined similar to a modern-day outhouse, one room for women and one for the men. The static-like feeling of the cold water splashing up on my arms from the forceful flow of the water felt refreshing. Captivated by my few moments of ease, I kept hearing the sound of a mannish sigh followed by a jerk, as the paper-thin wall vibrated from all the movement. I remembered a man following behind me as I was headed to the bathroom. The time between the sighs and the jerks got faster. As I was drying my hands, I realized it was one of the street peddlers who followed behind me to the bathroom.

When the *sigh, jerk, sigh, jerk, sigh, jerk* accelerated, it was a mystery no more. I wanted him to get an ear full of my disgust, so as I was leaving the bathroom I slammed the door. To make sure he got the message, I opened the door and slammed it again. In fact so hard, it gave off the sound of a violent earthquake. Suddenly the sound of racing hightops were upon me. "Are you okay?" Rashad said with a frantic look on his face.

"Don't fret, just needed to make a point," I shouted at the same time the peddler was coming out of the bathroom with a snake-like grin on his face. I had never seen Rashad so mad. "Man, what's wrong with you? Come here." The peddler's jacket ripped as Rashad clutched it with a tight fist and drug him towards the front door. I shook my head in disbelief while walking back towards the group to begin the meeting. Looking down at the trail marks left by the tip of the peddler's shoes as he was carried away so quickly, I couldn't believe someone could be so disrespectful and disgusting.

With the evening now drawing to a close, we all settled down to hear the concerns of the owners and the barbers. The meeting began with the sound of popping knuckles. "This meeting is about some new things that's going to take place around here in the next few weeks," Mel said to break the silence. Popping his neck, he continued, "Today is the day to say what's on your mind." I vaguely heard the terrorist introduction. I watched the homeless people walking by stopping to look through the large bay window, some thumping on the window to get attention and others looking for an extra buck to buy food. My heart connected with a woman walking by carrying a baby with a stockpile of beer cans.

There were more complaints from Mel than there was from anyone. Listening to him made me feel like my soul was having a stroke. I had met some interesting people over the years but I had never in all my life met someone so foolish. There are over six billion people on this earth and to even briefly think that you can treat all of them like rat droppings gives new meaning to the word *selfish*. "We ain't go keep opening this shop eight days a week if Toke is going to be the only barber that wants to work every day," Mel pouted, causing all eyes to focus in on me. My first thought was to tell him to go kick rocks. Considering that he was dumber than the back of a spoon, I relented.

"What about your customers, don't they matter? I arrive promptly on Sundays because they want me to be here," I said, now with all the crap I had put up with flooding my mind. "Who cares if it's one barber or ten barbers who arrive on Sunday? You all made the decision to include Sundays as one of the days that you will be open to provide services." To me it wasn't rocket science. "If you don't want to include Sundays as one of your days of operation, then don't. But to take it away because the person who is responsible for opening the shop is too lazy to do it is trifling," I said with a brave look on my face. There is nothing worse than listening to people complain about a situation that is within their control.

"Things don't have to be this way," I continued. "I am sick of hearing about the white man this and the white man that. The white man was not responsible for opening the shop at 8:00 a.m. You were, go figure. You treat people that look like you like they are nothing and blame it on what happened four hundred years ago. Come on man, catch up. Now that I've gotten that off my chest, let me tell you how you will treat me moving forward." I said all of that in one breath as the other barbers sunk down in their seats.

I then informed the owners that they were going to buy me a brand new barber chair, give me a key, and buy me a new barber station, or they could refund my money and I would work elsewhere. The barbers that had been there for years gave me a look that said, "I guess you better start packing."

When I returned to work on Monday, I had a new barber chair wrapped in a red bow and a new barber station with the countertop nailed down, and on top of it were four shiny gold keys. It is safe to say that from that day on all of the owners treated me like a queen. Unfortunately, the other barbers were upset and dumbfounded. The owners knew I was reliable and that next to their services, mine were the most in demand. And in a profession where most people are unprofessional and don't pay their rent on time, I did.

Two of the owners were spiritual dreads—Rashad and Solomon. I am not sure if they were Rastafarians, Christians, or Muslims. They never gave God a name. They referred to Him as supreme intelligence. As time went on they would leave literature, video tapes, and brochures on my station. It was information that was profound and somewhat deep to the average person.

One day I approached Solomon. "There are thirteen other barbers in this barbershop. Why do you leave this information only on my station?"

"Not everyone can handle knowledge. The thirst for knowledge is always fastened to the question, and people who are hungry for it don't just accept what they are told; they ask questions."

Rashad encouraged me to fast and pray. He always reminded

me that God is supreme intelligence, a love that surpasses all understanding and the image of equality. I listened to him and my life took
off. I was healthier than I had ever been in my life. I lost more than
seventy-five pounds. I walked every morning, saved lots of money,
read everything that I could get my hands on, and I figured out what
was missing in my life. It was self-discipline. The beauty was that
Rashad and Solomon did not teach me any more about religion than
I already knew. They taught me how to take responsibility for myself,
and they gave me information about the importance of showing God
respect by respecting all people. I learned how to show love toward
God by showing love toward people regardless of whether I knew
them or not.

Now that I had accomplished all my goals, it was time for me
to return home and start my own business. The customers were outraged that I was leaving. One of my customers, a district attorney,
grilled me when he found out I was leaving.

"Why would you want to go back to Nashville?" he asked.
"There is nothing there for black people. That's why they all come
here. You have done well here. I hope you don't think you'll do this
well in Nashville."

I felt like a deer in the headlights. *What if he's right?* Suddenly I
felt someone pulling on my sleeve. It was Rashad. He motioned for
me to come over to him. Rashad leaned toward me and whispered in
my ear, "What God has for you is in Tennessee. Go home."

I began packing that night. The next day the owner of the Nashville barbershop where I had worked called and asked if I would
manage her barbershop while she was out having a baby. I was reluctant because I wanted to start immediately on building my own barbershop, but I figured this would be great exposure for me before I
started my own business.

6

GOING HOME

"The simplest questions are the most profound. Where were you born?
Where is your home? Where are you going? What are you doing?
Think about these once in a while and watch your answers change."
—*Richard Bach*

I returned to Nashville in 2000. After a few months, I felt like I had gone back in time. Within the blink of an eye, I was back where I started—hanging out late with the same crowd and fighting the same temptations that I thought I had conquered. For some reason I thought since I had changed that they had changed that they had changed. Old habits had resurfaced but there was one thing that was different this time: I respected the fact that complete change takes time, and it doesn't always happen as quickly as we would like. There is a formula to complete change—it is called "process."

I had smoked marijuana before, of course, but this time something was different. It did not taste the same way it had in the past. One dark, chilly night when I was driving home, my eyes were red and glossy and my head was dizzy from the last puff of the joint. I started thinking about something that I had never thought of before. When I was high I would do my best to never let my mother or any other adult that I respected see me. As I stepped on the gas, I began to feel low on the inside, not because I was disappointed with my actions but because I never considered God's feelings about my actions. My heart began to sink deeper as if it were pressing through my back. Then I felt guilty because I hadn't kept my part of the deal. My mind raced from the vision of my dying in a car accident and showing up at God's door reeking like a skunk and my fingertips stained chocolate from smoking a roach. My heart felt like a thousand pieces of shredded paper.

I don't want to meet God high, I thought as I squeezed the steering wheel.

When I lived in Atlanta I had learned how to resist smoking marijuana by learning to say "no" because I didn't want to pay for it. In hindsight, I saw that I had learned how to deal with this situation on the outside but not from the inside. The thought of meeting God high and not knowing if I would live past my last mess-up changed me completely. I couldn't get that image out of my mind, and I didn't want to risk its happening to me.

But change can be depressing when you hang out with people who view change as something you do because you are not happy being yourself. They don't realize that change is your only option when you're not happy because you're not being your best self.

The environment at the barbershop was the same—riddled with the same loud, opinionated people with the same views that they had twenty years ago. The peddlers were still on schedule, and they even started their sentences with the same words: "I got the hookup." I knew then it was time for me to create an atmosphere that would make me and my customers happy.

One night I fell back into the sofa with a lot on my mind. I sat there staring at the ceiling and thought that things didn't have to be this way. I was frustrated because I didn't know how to make things happen. I cried and the hopelessness seemed like extra pounds on my lap. Something inside of me said, *Cry out to me. Yell, scream, or whisper if you have to. Toke, cry out to me.* I did not have the energy to yell or scream. "God, I want out," I said softly. "I do not want to live like this." Overwhelmed by the moment, I pushed myself up from the sofa and walked to the bathroom. I wanted to look in the mirror and see my face when I said it. "I don't want to live like this." The heat from my breath steamed the mirror. My right hand served as the windshield wiper as I wiped the thin mist off of the mirror, causing a squeaky sound. I wanted a second look, so I said it again. " I don't want to live like this anymore. If you don't want to live like this, then you have to be willing to completely change, even if every single person you know makes a choice to never change. Your lesson for today is accepting that change is *personal*," I said to myself in a motherly tone, as if I had a split personality. Finding myself back where I had started years ago made me want to vomit. I had been back in Nashville for only a year, but I had already let friends and family borrow all the money I had saved. I was at a dead end. But this experience taught me that God makes dead end visits if you request them. I took a deep breath and after letting it all out, I began to talk aloud.

"God, I have $3 and some change to my name, but if you give me a date I'll tell Tonya tomorrow that I am leaving to start my own barbershop." After a date popped into my head, I knew it was time for action.

When I woke up the next morning, I felt the butterflies in my stomach jumping around. In my head, a constant reminder shouted that all I had was $3 and some nickels and dimes. However, there was one valuable lesson that I learned while living in Atlanta:

Encouraging myself was my responsibility. I did this by talking to myself. When you talk to yourself, your heart listens as your brain thinks—both captivated by your willingness to include them in the conversation. When you encourage yourself, the answer you are seeking comes to you just like clockwork. I must admit that encouraging myself did not alleviate the fear that comes with complete change. But my desire to live better was greater than the fear of staying the same. Sure, I beat myself up for falling back onto a familiar path. My next thought was *Get up, get out, and get something!* In a split second, a comforting statement made by Margaret Thatcher found its way to my soul: "You may have to fight a battle more than once to win it."

As I drove to the barbershop, I felt happy because I had made a quick decision. In the past making decisions wasn't so easy. I had half a pack of smokes resting on the front passenger seat and enough money to buy a Happy Meal. By the time I arrived at the barbershop, I had one cigarette left. I was itching to smoke it, but the dizziness from the last five made it impossible. The atmosphere in the barbershop was relaxed because it was a cool day in July. Nashville was a college town and most students were moving back home.

Finally, I got the courage to invite Tonya outside to share my master plan that was backed by nothing but pure faith. How did I know it was faith? You know faith is operating when what you want is visible only to your mind and you leap anyway with the assurance that things will be found just as they were pictured in your mind. I told her that October 13 would be my last day and that I'd be opening my own barbershop on October 16. I could see the shock on her face; she thumped the ashes from her cigarette and paused. "I have one question for you, Toke: what would you do if you had to come back?" She then took a second pull from her cigarette and folded her arms. When she asked me the question I felt like something on the inside of me was released, I could see balloons of all colors sailing up towards the sky contained within each one was all my prayers, all my tears. Before I rendered my response, I thought about how her question to me was God's confirmation that my prayers had been answered. "No Tonya, I will not be back." I trusted heaven, and when heaven closes a door no man can open it. My time was up there and I accepted it. Heaven had closed the door and I knew in my heart that I would not be back.

For three months straight, I worked three full-time jobs to save enough money to purchase what I needed for my new barbershop: furniture, equipment, and filing cabinets. To my surprise, not sleeping in my bed for three months did not distract me from my ultimate goal. When the exhaustion of hard work became overwhelming, I thought about a piece of advice that my barber instructor had given me a few years earlier when I was a student: "If you live like your friends won't for two years, you'll live like they can't for the rest of your life." So I kept climbing. I continued to work hard to get the business off the ground.

On October 16, 2001, Toke's Barbershop, located at 2209 Buchanan Street, Suite 130, Nashville, Tennessee, opened for business. Starting my own business was no easy task, particularly starting from scratch. Although the days were long and I was exhausted, my motivation fueled me. On the days that I grew tired and weary, I would focus on the big picture and remind myself that this was just temporary. I would tell myself, *I know it's hard Toke, but keep going forward because there is nothing back there for you.*

Even though I had been running the barbershop while Tonya was on maternity leave, there were still a lot of ins and outs that I had not included on my to-do list. My hidden costs were more than I had anticipated. The hidden costs are things you didn't know in advance. For example, before painting my first barbershop, I had never painted anything. The suite that I was renting was purple. One Sunday morning I painted the walls white. This took several cans of paint and a whole day. In spite of thinking that I had done an excellent job, I returned the next day to find that the walls had turned back to purple. I went to the home supply store to inquire about this mystery. I discovered that one coat of primer would have reduced my work by half. Again, hidden costs show up as you move along.

I wanted my barbershop to make a difference in the community by providing the customers resources that they could use at home or at the shop. Great service is what people wanted, and I soon learned that most people were willing to pay double for it. Of course, this included the haircut, but it also included the hospitality service that was lacking in most barbershops. There was a tendency to conform to tradition instead of implementing a standard that made people feel comfortable. The tradition in most barbershops at the time reflected an aura of disrespect: Barbers ate lunch while serving the customer or took long breaks to talk to friends. The two things that were most prevalent were cursing and peddlers selling their stolen wares. I was determined to treat people the way I wanted to be treated, so I refused to allow peddlers in my barbershop. This was not an easy task because for them it was business as usual, and they considered the area where my barbershop was to be their territory. But I was paying the rent so it was my territory. And besides if I ever got out of that lifestyle I would not run my life or my business that way. I was not about to break my commitment by giving in to someone selling spoons. My customers wanted a haircut, not someone standing over them swinging open a jacket filled with tarnished gold bracelets.

I quickly developed a large clientele—including professional football players, council members, doctors, lawyers, television anchors, singers, and wonderful people from the community. At twenty-six, not only was I making a name for myself, but for the first time I was earning more than $1,000 a week. However there were some customers who were not happy with the new environment. They told me that my barbershop was the only shop that had a "no cursing" rule. I told them that I was twenty-six and they were much older and should know by now not to curse in front of women and children. I learned quickly that while rules ensure some form of equality for all, they often offend those who have no regard for anyone else's feelings. There was a place for people with this immature mentality, but it wasn't in my barbershop. While I was determined not to conform, I admit it was tough. One of the barbers who worked a few streets over told me years later that some barbers I had refused to hire said that I should "take my good-Christian ass and open up a church."

I had a cleaning service come in three times a week. My employees and I wore uniforms. Magazines were replaced by encyclopedias. I wanted to at least offer my customers the opportunity to use their time wisely while in my shop and gain something from the experience. I did not want them reeking of heavy cigarette smoke and their heads filled with "last night's lies." I was honored that of all the barbershops in Nashville where people could have spent their money, many chose to spend it in my shop.

It is not uncommon in a barbershop run by an African-American to have at least one person who talks too much, usually about nothing. It is as if they do not know it's okay to be quiet. Everything about a person who talks too much is harmful, even the advice they give.

As I focused on cutting my client's hair, one of the few customers that had a tendency to talk too much said, "Now that you own your own business you can come to work whenever you get ready." When the barbershop was empty that afternoon, I dropped to my knees and closed my eyes, allowing myself to go to a place of gratefulness. Whenever I was on my knees like this, my immediate thought was to do the opposite of whatever people suggested. If someone said to me, "You better stop working all those jobs. You're going to kill yourself," I would work even harder.

After I opened my business, I could afford to resign from both jobs, but I decided to keep the third-shift job working as a caregiver for individuals who were mentally challenged. This was my way of reminding myself that even though I owned my own business, I was providing a service to people. To perfect that service I had to learn to be wise and humble.

The transition from a job earning $7 an hour with a supervisor who treated me like I was a box of baking soda in the back of the refrigerator to my own business where I had the opportunity to implement my vision was an enlightening and humbling experience.

As I changed from my grave clothes to my clean, pressed barbershop uniform, my mind transformed as well. It became clear to me that how I lived my life could make a difference in some child's life. The thought of living my life in hopes of making a difference in the lives of children, including those not yet born, stayed on my mind quite often. There was a child out there who needed me to survive. I knew that because the women in history that I had read about as a child became my inspiration later in life. My courage to approach the barbershop owner with my idea to start my own business with only $3 plus some change came from the story of Mary McLeod Bethune. I read that she started Bethune College with less than $3. I thought surely if she can establish a college with less than $3, I can open a business. I read the story of Biddy Mason and Barbara Jordan to gather more strength. Their willingness to take the life they were born into and turn it into a life that they deserved inspired me

It also strengthened me to know that Oprah Winfrey was from Nashville and that she accomplished her dreams. I learned about Oprah in a strange way. Before 2001, I had not watched much of *The Oprah Winfrey Show*, but I had read about her in one of my black history books. One evening while shaving one of my customers who had a history of talking too much, the subject of Oprah Winfrey came up. This man had a mouth as foul as the sewage in the backyard, but his heart was as wide as the Red Sea. I tolerated him because he paid me $75 for a $5 shave. His only request was that during his appointments only he and I be in the barbershop. I also tolerated him because as off-base as he seemed, I thought he was interesting. He was as ignorant as they come, but he was as wise as you could imagine. He was a product of his environment, but he genuinely was a good person.

While I was massaging a hot towel into his beard, he began to tell me about my future. He usually talked about what happened to him in the 70s, what kind of car he had in the 80s, or who was shot in 89. But on this particular day it appeared that he had something he needed to get off his chest. As he talked with a toothpick poking out between his gold teeth, I listened.

"You remind me of that bitch named Oprah. In a few years, you'll probably retire from barbering and we will never see you again."

I knew in his own way he was paying me a compliment with the limited amount of words he had to pull from in his brain. His unexpected revelation made me stop. Barbering had been good to me. I couldn't see myself doing anything else.

Curious about his remarks, I asked, "What made you say that?"

Now with the toothpick relaxed on the left side of his cheek he said, "You know y'all like things a certain way. Since you opened your business, you have changed all the rules. No cursing. You can't stand outside and smoke a cigarette. At the rate you're going, soon we won't be able to talk."

When his words first registered, they hurt, not because I felt like he was putting me down, but because he could not understand that I put those measures in place to ensure that he had a positive experience at my barbershop. They also hurt because I knew Oprah Winfrey had been accused of things she never did. The accusations made against her were just inside the mind of the person who made them. Why did this hurt me? Because this was the only reality that I had ever known. It hurt because I knew what it was like to have to constantly fight to defend your character and reputation. Sometimes it can feel like you're breaking down when every time you turn around someone you helped or encouraged is making baseless accusations against you.

One day I had a customer steal $20 from me. I had taken off my smock to relax a bit because it was the end of the day. A few seconds later I went to the bathroom, and when I came back she was still standing at the counter. A moment later she left the shop. Once I got everything cleaned up, I sat down to recount my money. I had counted it before I went to the bathroom and to my surprise I was $20 short. Not only did she not come back to the shop, but she told other customers that I messed up her hair and that you couldn't pay her to visit my barbershop again. I knew what it was like to be accused not because a crime was committed, but in most cases just because I entered the room. After a while this became tiresome.

The customer's Oprah reference intrigued me, so I found myself tuning in to her show every day to find out why he had made the comparison. On the surface we did not have anything in common other than we both had cocker spaniels as pets. But my customer did not know about that. There was a twenty-year age difference between us. She was a talk show host, and I was a barber. She was a college graduate, and I only had a high school diploma. She was a billionaire and I was just progressing from a "hundredaire" to a "thousandaire."

So I started taking notes while watching Oprah. I noticed how she sat in her chair when she interviewed people. Whenever I was alone in the barbershop, I practiced sitting in different positions in my chair. Sometimes I held my breath for a few seconds trying to perfect the position because my legs were too big to rest comfortably on top of one another without snapping loose. I knew if I could master sitting on the big, clunky barber chair, I could sit on any chair like a lady. Also, I noticed that she had unpainted fingernails, and I was intrigued by her confidence to sport natural nails. Up until this day I was like most women, running to the nail salon to have my fingernails done on a weekly basis; my preference was the French manicure. Oprah's decision seemed to free me, and I no longer wanted to deal with the anxiety that comes with having acrylic flying across the room when I chipped my nail. Also, I no longer wanted to be a slave to feeling like I had to have my nails done once a week. The dust from the nail drill and the burning ammonia smell from the solution made evident why the technicians wore a mask, but it never made sense to me why they didn't offer the customers a mask if the fumes and chemicals were so harmful. From that day forward I have always sported my natural nails. I felt free.

The more I watched the show, the more I came to realize that his comparison was a compliment to both me and Oprah. He saw two women who wanted more. Neither of us had been sidetracked by our beginnings, and we had no intention of being stopped by the future.

From Oprah I learned how perseverance reveals a hidden beauty inside of you. Resilience trickled its way into her voice. Oprah's energy demonstrated that her life was in line with her purpose. I could hear "It is well with my soul" resonate from within her. During the commercial breaks, I would glance outside of my barbershop door that faced an alley. As I stared at the alley, I realized that Oprah had probably walked down some of the same streets I had. Oprah probably faced some of the same challenges that I had faced too. I believed that she had made a conscious effort to overcome them rather than blame others.

I had completed another step in my growth. No matter how much you think other people are to blame for your problems, they are not. You must take responsibility. Where you place the blame accounts for only 1 percent of life, and 99 percent is how you react to it. Oprah glowed with this knowledge and it revealed her inner beauty. Watching *The Oprah Winfrey Show* taught me the basics about business. Not only should you treat your customers like they matter, but they should also be considered in all of the plans that pertain to your business. Because I had no college education, she became my professor. And I must say she was a darn good teacher. I added another rule to my list: My customers were not allowed to bash Oprah in my barbershop. While my intentions were to be a great master barber, my life was shifting. My customers saw me as a leader.

I just wanted to provide my customers with great service and opportunities that were uncommon for a barbershop. I constantly looked for ways to make the experience better for my customers. I set up an area so they could apply for their voter registration cards. To my amazement, most of the people who complained about unfair elections and the newly elected officials had never registered to vote. It almost brought tears to my eyes when a man in his sixties, his oily face shining from a long day's work, knocked at my door within a few minutes of closing time. He wanted to register to vote. Even though I was probably forty years younger than he was, I understood why he was coming after hours. He was embarrassed. What is even more painful is that the very people who looked like him were the ones he was hiding from, not from the people he accused of rigging the election. One day while waiting to get his haircut he accused the new governor, who was white, of rigging the election. However, it was black people he was afraid would find out that at sixty-something he was not a registered voter. As I walked to the door to let him in, I was in awe of his courage. I admired him because during the course of the day he decided he wanted to make a change, but he did not want to be taunted for making a change.

At the time that I made my list of goals before moving to Atlanta, I thought my biggest achievement would be to open my first barbershop. I had no idea that I could make people look good and feel good, too, simply by reminding them that they are not alone; it is not too late; things don't have to be this way; you can have heaven here on earth if you treat people the way that heaven treats people— "equally." This was my biggest achievement.

Although this was my first business, I knew in my heart it would not be my last. I knew that every situation counted for something. Even the ones that made me feel lonely and awkward. Even the ones that made me appear to be this mean person who was withdrawn and introverted when in reality I was the opposite. I had my mind set on deliverance, and I knew that breaking generational curses of mediocrity, ignorance, and hatred would take more work on the inside.

One day I took a lunch break and decided to get a fish sandwich from one of the local restaurants. The place I went was a community staple and people flocked to it. That day as I was sitting at the drive-thru preparing to place my order, I was taken aback by something that I had seen several times before. But this time it was different or maybe something inside of me was different. Someone had written the words on the menu by hand. This restaurant had been in the community for more than thirty years. Didn't their customers at least deserve a sign that they could read? Then my next thought bumped out that one: *Your customer must complement your vision.* In other words, it is not enough to just have a vision. An entrepreneur must learn that although it is people who make the world go around, it is people who are like-minded that make your business go around.

Just looking at that menu made it even clearer to me that I wanted to give my customers more, but it would only be appreciated by those who wanted something better. I decided right then and there I was going to build a new barbershop from the ground up and give my customers something they had never seen before, at least not in Nashville. I felt it was the least I could do in return for the support that they had shown me over the years.

Again, I had no idea what I was walking into. But what I knew for sure was that opening my first business had broadened my view of things I hoped for. I was so excited about moving forward. As I focused on building the second barbershop, I also continued to perfect the first one. But there was one small lesson that I had to be reminded of. Over the years, I had learned that not all setbacks remind you of what you don't know or what you did wrong. Some reappear to remind you that there are some things to be learned as you go up the ladder. So don't be surprised when an unwelcome reminder comes knocking on your door.

I was at work one day when I heard the door chime. I glanced at the door, not really thinking much about the man's presence since we had a number of people in and out of the shop on their lunch breaks.

"Good afternoon," I said with a smile, taking in his sheriff's uniform. "Welcome to Toke's Barbershop. How can we help you today?"

"I'm here to pick up Chitoka Webb," he said.

Pick up? I thought. His announcement took me, along with most of the people in the barbershop, aback.

"Chitoka Webb," I said. "That's me. Pick me up for what?"

"There's a civil warrant for your arrest."

I didn't know what to say. I don't think I have ever been so embarrassed in my life. Here I was in my shop where my employees and our clients were present, including the client in my barber chair, and an officer was telling me he was here to arrest me.

"Why?" I asked, trying to sound as calm as possible. But my insides were doing backflips.

"You failed to pay for a gym membership," he said after consulting a piece of paper in his hand.

I racked my brain, trying to recall what he was referring to. I vaguely remembered having a gym membership years ago, but that place had gone out of business. He couldn't possibly be talking about it, or could he?

"Okay. So how do we handle this?" I wondered if I could just write him or someone a check to cover the outstanding amount.

"You have to go with me," he said.

I didn't have the nerve to look at the people in the shop. The backflips in my stomach turned to knots as I tried not to throw up. "Are you serious?" I asked, thinking there had to be some other way. It took me back to the time right after I had graduated from high school when I was forced to spend time in jail for driving without a license. Now, I vowed I would never be put in jail again.

Something inside of me knew this had absolutely nothing to do with the outstanding debt. I felt like this was just another dip in the road, to test me, to see how bad I really wanted to be successful. I knew I would pass with flying colors: I had already accepted in my mind that success of any kind takes a lifetime, so I was committed to the process. That still didn't stop me from being embarrassed. For most of my life, I had tried to stay away from bad situations and do the right thing. Now it seemed one small oversight was causing me public humiliation.

I kept my wits about me as best I could. I found the strength to face the people who were in the shop, and I gave a sigh of relief when my gaze landed on my cousin.

"Can you lock up for me?" I asked.

"Sure, Toke," he said, silently asking if I was okay.

I nodded and turned to the officer. "Okay, I'm ready."

He reached to his belt loop and removed his handcuffs.

I couldn't stop the panic from creeping into my voice. "Wh-what are you going to do with those?" I stuttered.

"I have to put these on you," he said. "Procedure."

"Are you serious?"

He almost looked apologetic as without another word he gently placed my hands behind my back and cuffed them together. Then he silently led me out to his police car.

How did I end up in this place again? I wondered as we headed toward the Criminal Justice Center. As though he was reading my mind the officer said, "God never gives us more than we can bear. Everything is going to be okay."

As much as I wanted to, I didn't believe him. How could everything be okay? I could only imagine what the patrons of my shop had to say after I left. I knew a couple of people in the neighborhood had witnessed the arrest. I was sure word would spread all over town. I visualized the headline of the next day's newspaper: SHOP OWNER ARRESTED WHILE CUTTING HAIR. I could also imagine the picture that would accompany it. It'd be one of me in shock, with my hands cuffed behind my back.

"It's going to be okay," the sheriff said again, eyeing me in the rearview mirror. "This is all part of a bigger plan. I don't know you, but when I entered your barbershop I noticed your taste for excellence. I have never in my fifty years seen a shop so peaceful. I could see my face in the floors they were so clean," he said as he laughed and gripped the steering wheel.

I looked at him thinking, *Thanks for the kind words.* While I deeply appreciated his comments, I was horribly embarrassed being led out of my business with these shiny little bracelets on in front of people who already despised me because I wouldn't participate in their stupidity because I wanted to feel right on the inside. *Thanks again, but you have no idea what my life will be like when I go back to work.* I looked down; the tears in my eyes were ready to spill out.

When we arrived at the jail, the sheriff let me out of the car and looked at me. "I'm going to take the cuffs off you," he said.

I smiled appreciatively, knowing he didn't have to do it. I rubbed my wrists as we walked toward the jail. Then he abruptly stopped as if he had been given direct orders.

"I normally don't do this when bringing an inmate in, but I'm going to take you through another entrance. It's used by the sergeants, sheriffs, and lieutenants."

I thought, *I really do appreciate your kindness and just wish it would have kicked in before you lead me out of the barbershop.*

When we entered his office, he pointed to a chair and said in a deep voice, "Sit down here. I am going to show you something that might keep you from getting yourself into this situation again."

He reached into his desk drawer, pulled out a Bible and laid it on top of a few stacked papers. I was eager to hear the lesson headed my way. Since childhood I have always had a love for learning, especially when the lesson was taught by someone older. While most kids were bruising their little fingers from twisting the horse-like hair of their plastic dolls, you could usually find me in the room with the senior citizens or in a daze from watching hours of black-and-white documentaries. For some reason this made more sense to me than what my peers were doing.

"Ms. Webb," he said, pulling me out of my daze as he licked his fingers and then flipped through the pages for a few seconds.

"Yes, sir."

He tapped the page several times indicating that he had found exactly what he was looking for. He looked up at me and read, "The wicked borrow and do not repay, but the righteous give generously."

"Pay your bills," he said sternly. "There is only one lesson to be learned here today. Whether this situation is eight years old or not, it is still unfinished. That is your lesson for the day. Pay your bills."

"Yes, sir," I said, nodding.

We made arrangements for me to pay the outstanding debt. Then we went our separate ways, but his kindness continues to stay with me. I had two choices: Either I could be upset that a bankrupt health spa sold its accounts to a group of attorneys who sued me for $382, or I could be grateful for the lesson. I chose to be grateful for the lesson.

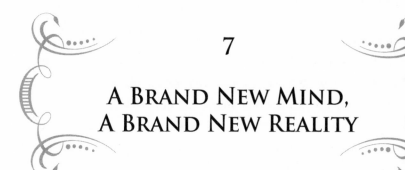

7

A BRAND NEW MIND,
A BRAND NEW REALITY

*"The illiterate of the 21ˢᵗ century will not be those who cannot read
and write, but those who cannot learn, unlearn, and relearn."*
—*Alvin Toffler*

Living your dream is nobody's business but your own. So put your
back into it, lean forward, and walk toward it because it is not going
to come chasing you down any time soon. Starting my first business
would teach me a valuable lesson; one that I would need to remember over and over again: "It all begins with you." Not your parents,
not society, or all the typical reasons people give for their failures. It
begins with an idea, a decision, and sometimes it begins with pain.
My life's journey has taught me that it does not matter where or how
you get started—just get started. Think about it. I got inspired to
build my second barbershop while on a short break to purchase a fish
sandwich. I became the most important person in a business setting:
the customer. You cannot understand your business until you learn
to understand your customer. I was ready for the biggest challenge

of my life: building the best barbershop in Nashville, one that would supersede my customers' needs.

Excited by my new idea, I raced back to the barbershop to suck my fish sandwich down before my next customer arrived. My mind felt like it was flipping over because of all the thoughts racing through it. *If I made it once, I could make it twice. But how?* It would take more than hard work this time. I had never purchased a home before let alone built a barbershop. Something inside of me knew I could do it. Even though I believed it too, I was in a daze trying to figure out where in the world to get the money to pull this thing off.

Chitoka, use what you have, I said to myself.

Self replied, *This time around it's going to take more than hard work and endurance.*

Ok self, now what?

Chitoka, you are going to need a brand new mind and a brand new reality.

But where do I start? This dream is bigger than the first one.

Building a barbershop from scratch is no different than repairing a building that is already standing, self replied. *Start where you are and with what you have.*

At the time I was still working the third shift as a caregiver at a local health-care agency while managing the barbershop during the day. I held on to this job as a reminder to remain humble and to teach myself how to juggle more than one thing at a time. If I wanted to be successful, I knew early on that this was crucial. Moonlighting as a caregiver is where my dream of starting my own health-care company began. This is how I would fund my new barbershop. In seconds I felt a boost of confidence come over me and my reality changed forever.

Working as a caregiver in a hospital, nursing home, or health-care agency is an entry-level position in a clinical setting. The duties of a caregiver usually involve the daily tasks needed to ensure the patient has a happy life. This can include bathing the person, cleaning up urine and bowel movements, doing laundry, preparing meals, and purchasing groceries. Sometimes you stroke the person's hair hoping to see them smile. Although the work was rewarding, the pay was not. But I was on a mission, and when you are on a mission, you don't get all bent out of shape about the process. Every step is taken with the end result in mind. This idea of building a new barbershop pushed me into overdrive. I thought about it while I was cutting hair. I thought about it while I was on my way to work at midnight.

I worked in a home with another caregiver. We both were responsible for caring for two individuals who were diagnosed as being mentally challenged. One night while reviewing the books in the home I wondered if I could own a company like this. I knew it was far-fetched and that the only people who would not laugh at my idea were the people I did not tell. All night long I read about the state and federal rules and guidelines, labor standards, and company policies and procedures. I also reviewed the plans that were developed for each patient by their social worker. My developing a health-care agency would definitely be a long shot. But it was too late because I already thought I could do it. Besides, from what I had read so far, I figured I had at least three good things going for me that were mandatory within the health-care field: I had a passion for helping people live better; I believed that all people were created equally; and my life's motto was to treat people the way that I want to be treated.

One morning at work, one of the members of the management team made an unannounced visit to the home. This was my chance to at least find out where to start.

I introduced myself before I could gather my thoughts.

"Hello, my name is Chitoka Webb," I said, showing all the teeth in my mouth. But hearing the door slam after my greeting made it obvious that my sheer presence was a bother. The manager's ragged attitude was a sign that she didn't want to be there. I was sure that she felt there was nothing more despicable than having a caregiver who makes $6.50 an hour asking stupid questions.

As I signed off on my daily charts I kept thinking, *I wonder if I can own a company like this.* Something inside of me said, *Sure you can. Now get back to asking more questions.* So I began to gauge the manager's temperament so I could pick the right time to get the answers I needed to start my own health-care agency. And that moment came when the manager sat down at the table to catch a breather from a long day's work by gulping down a cold glass of water. Without wasting any time I moved closer.

"What does it take to own a company like this?" I asked, showing all of my teeth for a second time. The bland look on the manager's face didn't reassure me that asking my second round of questions was the right thing to do. Right when I thought my choice to squeeze in one last question was a lost cause, the manager slipped me a note with the contact information of a co-worker who was known to help anyone in need.

As I made my way to the barbershop, I called him, told him my plans, and asked if he could help me or tell me how to get started. To my surprise, he said that he would be delighted to help me get started. I was so excited that I asked him again if he'd help me and when we could meet. "Sure, I will help you," he said. "I can meet you next week. You'll need to contact the Department of Mental Retardation to request an application."

Man, was I on cloud nine! In the mail a week later, I received the application to be a community service provider. The application was more than thirty pages long, but that didn't frighten me. It was the line in bold letters in the first paragraph that scared me: **It will take 8 to 10 months to complete this application**. *All right, Ms. Master Barber, let the show begin*, I said to myself. Even though I was excited, I was also afraid. I constantly pumped myself up. I decided I would do it afraid and never look back.

I worked on the application every day and every night. Sometimes I arrived at the barbershop at five o'clock in the morning for my clients who had to catch early flights. I had my clients scheduled every thirty minutes. I worked relentlessly like this until about seven or eight o'clock at night. Then I would leave the barbershop, eager to get back home to sedate my mind with the soothing voice of Nina Simone as I braced myself for another eight hours of trying to draft the perfect proposal. This was my schedule for the next twelve months. I kept telling myself it didn't matter that I managed a business and worked another full-time job. *Press on, push yourself, and relax and take a day off if you need to.*

Going full throttle twenty-four hours a day was beginning to take its toll on me, and I had accomplished my goal of learning to remain humble. So I decided to resign from my position as a caregiver. Now that I was free to work on my second business throughout the night, I was at it seven days a week.

I worked at the barbershop from 5:00 a.m. to 7:00 p.m. I scheduled appointments every thirty minutes, and occasionally I was able to take a walk-in appointment. I would leave the barbershop and head to Kinko's, sometimes arriving with more than $500. I went to Kinko's instead of using my home computer because I was 100 percent computer illiterate. I had purchased a refurbished computer a while back, but I was too embarrassed to tell anyone that I did not know how to turn it on. While Kinko's was expensive, I made it my nightly companion because I knew that being a twenty-something-year-old black woman without a college degree from the South, my application/proposal had to exceed the norm.

Some people might consider this reality unfair. Why couldn't I submit a basic proposal like everyone else? I don't know, and I did not care. Life is 1 percent what happens to you and 99 percent how you react to it. I chose to spend my time perfecting my proposal rather than giving in to the "poor me" voice. Upon arrival at Kinko's I would purchase a $100 card. Man! There was a charge for everything—talk about a la carte. There was a charge for printing, a charge for making copies, and a charge for working on the computer. I did this for six months and sometimes I would get frustrated because I'd make mistakes and have to start all over again. When that happened, I reminded myself about being on a mission and to not get bent out of shape about the process but to keep the end result in mind. Around 4:00 a.m. reality would set in when all my money was gone and I had to be at the barbershop in an hour. Some days I would leave Kinko's totally broke. On one occasion, I printed more than three hundred pages and had to reprint them because I forgot to put page numbers at the bottom. Mistakes were difficult for me because they were expensive. But I knew that my proposal had to be excellent because I did not want the review committee to know that I was a young, African-American woman who had no college degree. I wanted to qualify like all the other applicants. After a year of spending thousands of dollars at Kinko's and perfecting my proposal, I was ready to submit it.

The State of Tennessee review committee had three months to respond to my proposal. So I waited. I can't say that I waited patiently, but I waited! I was so anxious that I checked the mail on Sundays even though I knew that the carrier never delivered mail on

Sundays. I figured it couldn't hurt. To this day, I can still remember dropping my head each time I closed the door to that narrow, little mailbox; the smell of its four corners was a swift reminder that it was empty! But I could not give up. Not because I wasn't tired, but because I did not know how to. All I had in me was fight. I was determined to fight until the end.

The funding for the new barbershop would prove to be a challenge as well. I applied for a $10,000 loan and my bank denied it. Then I applied for a U.S. Small Business Administration loan for $15,000. It was denied. Then I applied through another bank for $15,000 and was denied again. Interestingly enough, after the last bank denied me, they referred me to another financial institution that helped business owners like me who did not have strong enough credit to get approved through a bank but had the assets and earning potential to secure a small loan. Needless to say I applied through this institution and received a loan for $26,100. After being denied so many times, I created a folder in my filing cabinet and labeled it "Denial Letters." I knew my faith would not let me down but I also knew that prayer was not a substitute for hard work, so I began to keep every denial letter that I had received from any project that I was working on. Then I decided to start filing acceptance or congratulatory letters behind them. So I added the approval letter from the bank—filing it behind the three denial letters that I had received the first time around.

Every accomplishment was "yes, you can" receipt. Some took longer to achieve than others, and along the way I discovered something about myself that I never knew or just never noticed before. I had a passion for creating. Once I realized I had the power to create good things—things that people could use to make their lives better—my endurance tripled. From then on, when I encountered a battle, I would not just think of myself, I would also think of people who could learn from the trials and tribulations of my journey. So I would fight harder.

As I began to work with the developer to lay out the new barbershop, I was amazed by how we developed the initial plan.

"Okay, young lady, I want you to get a piece of notebook paper and draw out to the best of your ability the vision that you have in your head," the contractor said as he squinted at me. "And make it plain! Don't get frustrated with it. That's my job."

I thought to myself: *With all the skyscrapers built in this world, this was the first step: simply drawing it on a piece of paper. Wow, now I really can do anything!*

On the way home, I stopped at Wal-Mart and bought the biggest notebook known to man. I know it weighed five pounds. I did exactly what the developer asked me to do: draw my vision of the barbershop and keep it simple.

Even though I was developing a new barbershop and creating a health-care agency, I still had to focus on my current barbershop. I made a promise to myself that while I was building the other two businesses I would not let anything affect the standards at Toke's Barbershop. This was my beginning, my foundation. Something inside of me said, *Do not despise small beginnings.*

In April 2003, after checking my mailbox for 159 days straight, I finally received my first response from the state. Once I got inside my house, I took a couple of deep breaths and opened the letter with confidence. It said my proposal had been denied because neither I nor my principals had enough management experience in the mental retardation field. I was devastated. I fell back in the chair and without rhyme or reason I said, "Not this far." I had spent an entire year just completing the application and spending all my money night after night at Kinko's.

Something inside of me said, *Settle down and read the letter again.* So I read it again. It was painful to read the word *denied.* Then it dawned on me—denied doesn't mean never. Remember the situation with your high school graduation. Denied does not mean never. Give them what they are asking for by finding someone who has management experience in the mental retardation field. So the woman I had slated as the board chairperson I moved to executive director, and I remained as the chief executive officer. Once I made those changes, I resubmitted the proposal. Even though I knew I'd have to wait another three or four months to get a response, after the third week, I was back checking the mailbox on a daily basis.

I couldn't sustain this because my attention for the next few months had to be on the interior design of the barbershop. In my mind, I kept seeing earth-tone colors, leather furniture, handmade barber chairs, massage chairs, stone tile, a private reading room, and lots of windows. The ideas were plentiful; they usually are when your goal is for the common good. I must admit though, while it was fun, it was also hard work. After working at the first barbershop for ten hours, I would then head to the new one and paint for hours. In the end, I had to pay a professional painter to complete the job once again. But after months of working with plan developers, builders, city inspectors, and all the other people in between, my dream of a state-of-the-art barbershop became a reality. And it was everything I had envisioned. On June 9, 2005, the new Toke's Barbershop opened for business.

Now that things were running smoothly, I focused my attention on developing my first health-care agency. Within three months of resubmitting my proposal, I received a phone call requesting a meeting with me and my team. I was excited. I remember being so excited that I wanted to shout: "Finally, after spending a year completing the application and spending six months going back and forth with the state, they want to talk to me. And by all means, I want to talk to them!" I was so excited that I was not sure if my nerves could stay put until the appointed time to meet with the state representatives.

On a quiet Monday morning, I was resting as I often did because my shop, like most barbershops, was closed. I was awakened by the faint sound of a phone ringing, and to my surprise it was one of the state representatives I was scheduled to meet with the following week. She informed me that the new person I had listed as the director was considered a conflict of interest. I was not sure where the conversation was going.

"Are we still scheduled to meet next week to discuss the contract?" I said in a confused tone.

"No, we will send you a letter in the mail."

As quickly as the phone call started, it ended. I wanted this contract really badly but I realized that if I was not careful, I could mistakenly allow this dream of owning a health-care company to define me. I had done a lot of self-evaluation and healing over the years, and I knew the negative effects of allowing monetary things or notable achievements to define me as being successful. I silently reminded myself: *You are not of this world. Remember you're on a spiritual journey.* This is peace in its truest form! When I received the letter, it said the state had now denied my proposal twice and a provider can apply only three times. In other words, I had one more chance. But as far as I was concerned that was all I needed—another opportunity. So I submitted my proposal a third time. It didn't bother me that if they denied me this time I could never submit another proposal. Actually I was excited by the challenge. I was more pumped under pressure than I was when it looked promising. I prayed constantly for guidance on getting approved the third time around.

Later that evening, I did what I always did when faced with an unexpected setback. I got up, got moving, and got to thinking. I decided that I would take a drive around town in complete silence. I pressed the window controls repeatedly to keep out any sound of the wind as I made my best attempts to draw in the wisdom needed to devise my next move. I knew it wasn't going to be easy, and I was running out of ideas. Then I thought, *What's with all the worrying? Nothing has been easy but you made it this far. Do what you did the last time*, landed in my mind like an airplane dropping from the sky. So I found someone with the same management experience as the previous executive director, reorganized the board again, and called it a night.

I put the revised proposal in the mail the next evening. Four months later, I received the letter I had been waiting for. When I opened it, the first word that I saw was one I hadn't seen in the other letters: Congratulations! After two years of filing papers and negotiating, it was official. I was on my way to developing my first successful health-care agency.

Life was sweet. By the time I'd turned thirty, I had started three businesses. And I wanted to do even more. I could not stop. I felt like there was more in me. I hired a young lady to research other states to see if there was a need for more health-care companies to provide services for the mentally challenged. After a few months of searching, she discovered that Alabama needed more providers. So I started developing my fourth company, and I flew to Alabama to attend an orientation for new providers. I had the pleasure of meeting Ms. Mitchell, the regional director for Alabama's Black-Belt counties, which were poor and rural.

Once the orientation was over, I introduced myself and told her that I was interested in developing a health-care agency in her area.

"Can you tell me how to get started?" I asked as she stared at me.

"You seem mighty young," she said. "Is it just you, or are you with a group of people?"

"Do you mean did I travel with someone, or do you mean do I have business partners?"

"I mean do you have business partners," she said.

"Well, I don't have any business partners but I do have a partner," I said as I pointed toward the ceiling.

She smiled as if she knew where I was coming from. "Yes, Ms. Webb, we do have a need in my area, and now we have the funding to bring in more providers."

She told me to get more information and the application from the state's website, complete it, and then call her so we could meet. I shook her hand and thanked her. I completed the application in a few months and gave Ms. Mitchell a call. She informed me that the funding was no longer available but that I could still fly down and meet with her if I wanted to. Of course I wanted to meet with her, I was on a mission and when you are on a mission you don't get all bent out of shape about the process. We agreed on a meeting time, and I could tell that she was trying to see if I was serious or just another person who had no intentions of doing anything but just asking questions.

When I arrived at her office, she met me with a wide grin and said she was glad I could make it. She glanced at a piece of paper in her hand and told me that she had made a mistake and that there was funding for new providers. My heart pounded from hearing what I thought was good news.

"So funding is available for me to start developing my health-care company here in Alabama?" I asked her.

She showed me the paper and told me to look at line two where it stated that there was funding. We looked at each other and smiled.

"So what's the next step?" I stood up because I was ready to take off and get to work.

"Your application had already been approved, and now I'm signing off on it and will send it to the federal government. Once we get the contract signed, we will call you and schedule an appointment for you to meet with the entire regional team."

I shook her hand and thanked her. "I appreciate the opportunity and don't hesitate to contact me if you need any more information."

"Congratulations, Ms. Webb," she said. "We'll be in touch."

As I was walked down the steps, I thought to myself, *If you can make it once you can make it twice.*

My drive home was joyful. I drove the entire trip in silence so I could hear all the thoughts in my heart dancing around because of this new opportunity to create. In August 2006, I developed my second health-care company in Alabama. Life was getting sweeter by the minute. Years of hard work were once again so paying off. Everything around me seemed to be shining as though the universe was smiling at me.

One thought resonated through my mind that day: *I am glad to be me.* My position as the CEO of two companies taught me another whole phase of being humble. Our society has been successful at painting CEOs as people who ride around in expensive cars with the sunroof opened talking on cell phones. What most do not see is the personal and financial sacrifices that CEOs make on a daily basis to ensure that their companies are successful. On one occasion, when the state unexpectedly cut the funding, I had to scramble to meet payroll, which totaled over $60,000 a month at the time. So I decided that I would use all of my personal savings to ensure that payment to the employees was not interrupted. I did not have one red cent left. I was able to put all of my bills off for thirty days due to my excellent payment history, but the gas company's policy did not allow customers to extend their bill past two weeks, so my gas was turned off. This was in late December, and it was one of the coldest winters in Tennessee. As I lay there night after night in my home with no heat in the freezing cold I thought about my employees, I thought about how some of them seek to destroy and tear you down, filing baseless labor claims and reporting false reports of abuse to draw in state inspectors. I thought about how sad it was when a group of people will join together to destroy the very company that provides a livelihood for their family but will not join together to build up other employees, build up the company.

As the tip of my toes turned numb from the frostbite-like air coming up through the vents, I began to think of the employees who were not like that, the ones that made the same personal sacrifices as I did because they believed in my company's mission. They believed in me, and they wanted to see all of us succeed. For them, if necessary, I would have gone another month without any heat. One of those people was a woman named Mrs. Thompson; she was the executive director. One day, after a four-hour board meeting, we were preparing to leave for the day. I thought everyone had left, so I walked to the back of the building to gather up all the small heaters that the team coordinator had purchased for the management team during a recent camping trip. While walking back to the front of the building I heard what sounded like someone shuffling keys. "Oh, Ms. Webb, I thought you had already left. Do you need some help carrying those heaters?" Mrs. Thompson said with a curious expression on her face.

"Sure, I could use a hand," I said. "I thought I could carry all five, but as you can see I do need a little help." I was praying she would not ask me why I was taking the heaters. She didn't. Instead, she made light of the situation. "I don't know what you're going to do with all of these heaters. But you'll be pleased—the heat is hot enough to cook a roast!" We laughed in unison and I breathed a sigh of relief.

Having a little heat allowed me to sleep during the night without shaking from the cold. As I rose the next morning to sit on the side of the bed and let out my morning yawn, my breath produced a small white cloud of smoke. My mouth was warm but my bedroom was not. Fortunately, the next month, the funding did return. I made it through without any of the management team knowing what had happened, being a CEO is not something that you wake up and decide to do. For me, it happens to be a part of my journey. A journey that I did not design, but one that I accepted.

8

I NEVER SAW IT COMING

"It always seems impossible until it is done."
—Nelson Mandela

As one of my employees approached my door, I didn't think her visit would be any different from any other interruption throughout the day. Little did I know what was lurking right around the corner. As I rushed to complete a last-minute report, the stress stretched the skin on my face and caused the sweat to drip off the tip of my nose. I was so hot. I'm sure the employee could see steam rising from beneath my blouse. I felt like I was going to explode from the pressure of trying to do a good job. It wasn't the first time I had been stressed out, but this time I was more than stressed. It made me think of an example my seventh grade teacher, Mr. Johnson, gave once about how pressure bursts pipes. My hands began to swell like a rubber latex glove filled with water as I pushed each finger to the max.

I typed as fast as my fingers could move, periodically looking from the computer screen to the paper beside me. My office was extremely quiet. The only distraction was the silent sunlight shining through the window behind me, warming my back and making me sleepy. But I continued typing. I had no clue that with each keystroke I was getting closer to something that would forever alter the course of my life. I remember not having a care in the world that morning. I was twenty-nine-years-old, the owner of a new barbershop and the CEO and founder of two health-care agencies. I had just purchased my first home. And three weeks earlier my doctor had pronounced me to be 100 percent healthy during my annual physical examination.

"So doc, considering that I'm 100 percent healthy, what would you recommend I do to keep it that way?" I said in a childlike voice.

While I was extremely successful, nothing pleased me more than being healthy. He peeked at the clipboard, thumbed through a few of my test results and squinted as if he was about to give me top-secret CIA advice. "Keep doing what you've been doing."

Overall, I was at a good place in my life. Years of sacrifice and struggle had come full circle. I had finally reached a point in my life where I truly believed any experience, good or bad, could not ruin my inner peace and gratitude without my permission. I believed everything happens for a reason and the lesson was more important than the reason. I understood rather quickly that reasons can be tied to other people's motives. But when you choose to learn the lesson it becomes yours forever. This confirmed my belief that if I allowed my trials and tribulations to run their course, ultimately they would make me a better person.

As the echo of footsteps drew closer to my office, I typed faster because I wanted to out-type the interruption I knew was headed my way.

"Good morning, Ms. Webb," the employee said respectfully. "I don't mean to bother you."

"Oh, no problem, Brenda," I said. "You're not bothering me at all. How can I help you?"

I hit the last keystroke to finish my report. And filled with excitement, I looked up for her response. That's when everything changed.

I tried not to let my panic show as I looked in the direction of Brenda's voice. I couldn't make out her features or the color of her clothes. It was just the fuzzy silhouette of a person. I blinked and blinked hoping things would be clear again. I could hear the pen in my hands slightly cracking from the pressure of my grip. That was not enough to ease my feeling of despair, so I began to tap my feet. *Holy crap, I can't see a thing!* I tried again to blink my sight back but it did not work. I couldn't see anything. It was like looking through a window smeared with gunk. My heart felt broken, almost as if the sadness were running down the middle of my chest. Life as I knew it was gone just that quickly! I never knew I could feel so many emotions within five seconds. I felt alone, miserable, confused, sad, dazed; I didn't know whether to have a nervous breakdown or to just die. My mind was racing along with my heart; each beat felt like it was pushing through my silk blouse.

"I'm here to pick up my monthly forms," Brenda said.

Thoughts raced through my mind as I tried to remain calm. But truthfully I was more frightened than I had ever been in my life. My heart continued to pound and my pulse thickened in my throat. *I'm going blind. God, please help me,* I silently prayed. The thought of going blind tore through my self-worth like a tornado tears through an old log house in the country plains of Oklahoma.

Despite the emotions raging through me at that moment, an image of me as a child living in the housing projects flashed before me. I was seven years old and it was the first day of school. A little boy and I were bouncing a ball back and forth. Everything around me seemed to be shining as though the universe was smiling down on me. I remember one thought resonated through my young mind that day: *I am glad to be me.* Despite the shift that had occurred in the blink of an eye, surely if I could encourage myself at the age of seven, I could convince myself at the age of twenty-nine that everything would be just fine. I was determined I was going to finish the way I started. I was going to continue to be *glad to be me.*

Brenda thanked me for my time and retrieved her forms. I quickly rubbed my eyes, hoping things would be clear again. To this day I still hold on to that wishful thinking. Even now I can feel the wind that rushed in when Brenda closed the door. I knew then that the intercourse between the disease and my eyes were forever intertwined. The closing of the door reminded me of the last scene in Michael Jackson's "Thriller" video where the door sounds like its being ripped from latches that haven't been oiled in centuries. Despite the eeriness of it all, the closing door brought some measure of relief. I had remained calm. Brenda never knew that I was suddenly lost and frightened. I was the CEO of the company, but like most leaders, I was more concerned with her well-being than my own.

I learned long ago that leadership is an action not a position. And even though everyone thinks you're the strongest person in the room, life has a way of reminding you that you are just an ordinary person. At that moment I was lost and confused. No longer being able to see, I wanted to fall to my knees and scream out the pain, but something inside of me kept my body standing. My next thoughts were *Use your hands, make a move, call somebody.* After I picked up the phone, feeling for the numbers gave me the hope I needed to keep going. Before this tragic moment, it was look and see. Now it was touch and see—touching became my sight. While this was a good starting point, I was a wreck, and I just wanted to feel safe. I wanted nothing more than to run into the arms of someone who would protect me from the pain and the apprehension.

This is not the ending that I had played out in my mind over the years. This is not how my life was supposed to end. From childhood to adulthood I had one simple prayer and that was that I would never get sick. I had lived long enough to see cancer eat the bones of good-hearted people, strokes paralyze bodies and turn smiles upside down, and multiple sclerosis ravage the muscles of people who walked daily and watched what they ate. I had seen a debilitating disease so powerful that it shattered the dreams of a family within seconds.

I knew I had to call someone quickly. I needed to call someone who would not panic like me. Someone whom I trusted with my fears and my insecurities. As a self-sufficient, highly confident business leader, I felt that there were very few people I could call and say, "I'm afraid and I don't know what to do. Oh yeah, and please help me!" So I called my spiritual advisor at the time.

"Ms. Toke, you need to get to the eye doctor right away." His thick bohemian accent hung on each word. This was his way of telling me now's not the time to play superwoman! "Stay right there," he said. "I'm on my way to get you."

I had already gathered what I could and I was ready to go. "I have to get out of here now," I squealed. "It's getting worse." I was losing control and not thinking straight.

"And, Ms. Toke, how are you going to get to the doctor if you can't see clearly?" His low voice made him sound like a pleading father. He knew that when my mind was made up, there would be no changing it.

"I am going to drive," I said as if his question was silly and my answer was obvious.

As an entrepreneur, I have never had the luxury of wasting time or weighing risks. So I did what I had always done when life seemed to be too much to bear: I got up and got moving. I cannot remember where I learned this, but I know it's always worked for me. So I made my way to my office door and then to the building entrance. I felt the walls and focused on what was directly in front of me. As often as I'd gone in and out of my office, I never knew what the walls felt like. As smooth as the paint looked, when I got to the end of the wall, my fingertips were throbbing from rubbing the small bubbles in the paint.

I had a short walk to the car, and I stayed along the edge of the concrete, which ended where my car was parked. Just to make sure I had the right car, I ran my hand across the hood to feel for the BMW emblem. My car was an alpine white, which made it easier to see, though it was a total blur. But the keys worked so I knew it was mine. After I started the car, I began to have second thoughts. Maybe I should have someone drive me to the doctor. Something inside of me immediately argued, *I don't want to sit here and wallow in this pit of blurriness. Put the car in reverse and let's get help. This is not the first time you've had to make a hasty decision with few resources. Now get with it and let's get moving.*

Before I put the car in reverse, I told God, "I know this is crazy, but trying is all I know." As the car softly jerked back, I pondered my decision again to make sure I could live with the consequences. I could, so I started driving. I opened all of the windows so I could hear clearly. I didn't know how I was going to do it, but I knew I had to do it. It was like driving in a fog. The closer the object, the easier it was to identify. My natural senses became my greatest asset. I trusted them enough to lead the way during this crisis. I quickly figured out how to maneuver with limited vision and with the help of my mind reassuring me that everything would be fine as long as I listened to the sounds that surrounded me. It helped that I was familiar with the area, had had 20/20 vision for twenty-nine years, and was only forty-five minutes into this trial.

While driving to the doctor, I rode in the slow lane. I could feel the old lady poking me in my side laughing. All those years I had thought she drove in the slow lane because she couldn't keep up! Oh, how the tables had turned! Now I realized she couldn't see. When I reached the doctor's office, I silently thanked everyone who drove in a patient manner and obeyed the traffic regulations. Unbeknownst to them, they helped lead me safely to my destination.

My doctor, Peter Van Hoven, was the happiest doctor alive. His energetic aura could make a person with no legs do a backflip. Being positive and uplifting was part of his personality. When he examined me, he was so positive that for a moment I thought going blind was a good thing. I was waiting for the confetti and the balloons to fall from the ceiling. He kept smiling even when he told me that I might go completely blind. His optimism was contagious, and I almost forgot I could hardly see.

Dr. Van Hoven identified the disease as Panuveitis, for which there is no known cause. It can affect anyone at any age, but it is most commonly seen in women who are in their forties. It is the leading cause of blindness in the world. He informed me that the disease had probably been in my body for about two years and that it would require medication. He prepared to load my eyes with steroid drops and explained that it looked like someone had smeared grease on my eyes.

Due to the severity and the rate of deterioration, my doctor referred me to a retina specialist immediately. The first available appointment was for Monday morning. As he tilted my head back to put the steroid drops in, I tried to keep still, but my hands clutched the leather armrest. The soft leather pressed against my fingernails as I dug in. The solution covered my entire eye like glaze on a sweet lemon cake. After he finished he said, "Chitoka, close your eyes and sit here for about forty-five minutes." I swallowed a gulp of air, expressing my impatience. "Forty-five minutes," he said with a laugh and then left the room.

Forty-five minutes felt like an eternity but the medication worked. Before I opened my eyes, I could feel the doctor smiling at me.

"I think you're ready," he said. "Let's take a look."

I popped my eyes open, and I could see his face. It wasn't as clear as I would have liked but I could see. I informed the doctor that I had plans on Friday to travel to Georgia for a women's retreat. He advised me not to attend or to make any arrangements until I met with the retina specialist on Monday. As I sat in the doctor's office long enough for the steroids to take their course and restore my sight I knew I would disregard his instructions. After the steroids had taken their course, I wiped the milky substance from my eyes and went off to make travel plans. Since the medication allowed me to see fairly well, off to the retreat I went. And I decided to drive alone. I prayed for traveling mercies and no surprises.

Though I got there safely, on the second day my eyes turned red and glossy. I had to squint to see clearly. I knew I was in trouble when I mistook the female room attendant for a man. Later that night, after one of the workshops was over, I was walking to my car when I heard someone walking on the sidewalk in the distance, but I couldn't see them. Although I could tell from the quiet that it was just one person, I could not tell if it was a man or a woman until he brushed by me and I heard what sounded like a gush of wind blowing forcefully through a small bush; his heavy breathing came out with a force and got trapped in his mustache. He was breathing hard. I was listening for his footsteps to stop to see if he was going to turn around and walk toward me. I am sure he knew I could not see him since I almost walked right into him. When I finally made it to my car, I said to myself, *Something is really wrong.* And myself replied, *Did the doctor tell you not to come for his health or yours? . . . Hell yeah there is something wrong!*

Fortunately, my mentor was a facilitator at the retreat. She was kind enough to cancel her flight and drive with me back to Nashville. On the way home, I turned the road signs into an eye exam. My disbelief turned into laughter. Sometimes, shedding pain in the form of laughter is a lot nicer to the soul than shedding pain in the form of those salty, crystal-like drops that spill from your eyes when your heart has been shattered. For me, having a visible illness made me feel like a failure. I did not want my mentor, of all people, to see me in this state. As we zoomed by each sign, I leaned over and asked, "Can you read that sign?" Her response was, "Uuuh, yeah. Can *you* read the sign?"

But we both knew that I was in the passenger seat for a reason. The greasy blur was slowly returning; everything I saw appeared to be covered in a thick layer of sap. I never told her, but my heart was crumbling by the minute. I was at a total loss that something like this could happen to me so suddenly; it was quick like death—no time to think, no time to wonder, and barely enough time to accept it. My life was peaceful. I did not understand how this weirdness was going to fit in, so I kept telling myself that I could see. It would have hurt too much to believe otherwise. If someone had asked how I was, my response would have been, "I'm fine. I can see!" If someone had asked me, "How is your day going?" I'd have responded the same way. "I'm fine. I can see." It was obvious I was trying to convince myself. However, I've learned that people prefer the real you.

I knew that whatever this disease was, I'd need everything inside of me, including wisdom, faith, and a little wine at times to help me persevere through this stage of my life. I reflected on past situations that looked like complete failures but had amazingly positive outcomes. Somehow I had made it through those experiences without a scratch, and now I reflected on those joyous moments in time where I had accomplished the impossible to push myself forward. As I reflected, I knew there were more occasions than I remembered and that these joyous moments had been going on for a long time.

The first moment that came to mind was when I was five years old. It was 1979, and we were living in the Preston Taylor Housing Projects. As a child, there were many rules that were not to be broken without severe consequences. I had to be in the house before dark, and I couldn't leave the front yard. On this day, I got an uncontrollable taste for hot, moist chocolate brownies, the kind that dissolve in your mouth. I came up with a master plan and a way to carry it out before anyone would notice. Unlike today where you can find tons of bakeries, in the housing projects our bakery was at Ms. Smith's house. I had my plan and my time frame, and I knew which way to go. But I did not know which apartment was hers. As I walked, I noticed a fat man with broad shoulders walking towards me. "Hello, where are you going so fast?" he said as he stooped down in slow motion to look me in the eyes. Looking up at him forced me to hold my head all the way back as if my neck were broken. "I'm going to Ms. Smith's house." All I could think about was those hot, moist chocolate brownies. He extended his hairy hand. It was big; it reminded me of Godzilla, so I stepped back and put my hands in my stained yellow shorts. I had gotten them dirty earlier from rolling down the hill. "Oh I'm sorry, I didn't mean to frighten you," he said as he grinned and looked around the corner. "What's your name?"

I really believed he was sorry. "My name is Toke." I'm not really sure why, but I'd always trusted men with gray hair. Maybe because I trusted the men at church, and all of them had gray hair. " I got two quarters." The soft breeze from the settling of the sun rushed into my mouth, through the gap left by my missing three front teeth, causing my gums to tingle.

He put his hands in his pockets and said, "Come on Toke, I will take you there. Isn't that funny, I was headed that way too." I trusted him. He smelled liked the pastor at church, and his eyes were no longer moving quickly side to side. I accepted his invitation and began to walk behind him as he led the way. As we walked down the curvy sidewalk something inside of me didn't feel right. He kept looking back at me, and there is nothing that unnerves a sassy little girl than someone staring at her. Once we arrived, the setting began to look familiar. However, what concerned me was he was leading me to the back door instead of the front door. He walked up onto the back steps. "Come on Toke, this is it." Little did he know that I had always gone through the front door. I didn't even know that there was a back door. As I walked behind him, I noticed that no one else was back there. My heart began to race fast like that machine momma uses to whip potatoes. The quarters smushed in between my fist were soaking wet, and everything around me felt busy. Something was trying to tell me something. Immediately something inside of me said, *Turn around and run as fast as you can.* I ran so fast my shoes flew off. Needless to say, I did not get my brownies, but I did get a second chance at life.

Although I had treaded the waters of relationships, finances, and plain old life experiences over the years, diseases, illnesses, and disorders were unfamiliar waters in my life. Just like nature, they do not take names or provide you with an introduction. Their only objective is to finish the task at hand. Before the weirdness of this disease, a normal week for me was business meetings, lots of reading, traveling, mentoring, advising others, and being advised and mentored myself. The weeks after the blindness took up residence in my body consisted of at least five doctor visits every week, different kinds of medications, eye injections with a needle long enough to use as a microphone, and eye drops. (I was told that if I used one after the expiration date, it would glue my eye closed.)

One evening at the barbershop, I was finishing my last customer, my mentor, when she looked at me like a concerned mother and said, "Excuse me, Ms. Webb, why are your eyes so red?" I could tell by the look on her face that this needed my immediate attention. While walking to the bathroom, the gust of wind from my stride caused my eyes to feel like they had been scorched. I never noticed it throughout the day because I had stood in one place for sixteen hours cutting hair. When I reached the bathroom and turned on the lights, for a second I thought someone had thrown fireworks into my face, the flash of the light coming on was piercing. I looked in the mirror, and my eyes were soaked in blood. They were so red that I could not see my pupils. I leaned closer to the mirror trying to find the little black pupil; I opened my eyes as wide as I could only to find a dot similar to a period. I knew something was terribly wrong, but I felt fine, so I brushed it off as stress from working such long hours. I had no idea that three weeks later my entire life would change forever. I never saw it coming!

During my barbering career, I was fortunate to meet Patricia Cunningham. She was the wife of one of my most loyal customers, and she would accompany her husband every now and then to the barbershop. Initially this was the only interaction that I had with Mrs. Cunningham. Her husband spoke often about his love for her; he seemed delighted about her being his first girlfriend and his only wife. One story in particular that warmed my heart was when he told me of all the preparation that he put into getting ready the morning that he took her to meet his mother. "I knew then that I would marry her," he told me. They had been together for thirty-three years. I didn't know much about her except she worked at a bank and was always vibrant and smiling. When she came to the barbershop with her husband, I jokingly thought that her mission was to get me to wrap the clipper cords around her neck and pull as tightly as possible. She would stand next to me and wipe his face, pointing out a spot I had missed. It did not matter that I had just started the haircut. He would just smile and say, "Now, Pat," and she would continue brushing his face. It was always a joy to see her.

One evening Mr. Cunningham came to the barbershop wearing dark shades and a baseball cap pulled down over his glasses. I knew something was wrong because he never wore his hat inside the building. As he was preparing for his haircut he began to cry.

"Pat's cancer is back," he said as his large shoulders jerked back and forth from the force of the tears now rolling over his cheeks. This was devastating news because it had been in remission for some years. It stayed on my mind the entire time he was at the shop and long after he left. My heart ached for him and her.

A few weeks later, I asked him if I could spend the night at the hospital without her knowing. I wanted to extend my help by sacrificing my time, and I did not want to disturb her. He accepted my offer and suggested that I let her know because it would make her happy. I arrived at the hospital with my overnight bags and some books for reading. When I walked into her room, she looked at me as if I were William Shakespeare. It was evident that she was confused by my presence, but very polite and appreciative of my visit. I told her I did not want to disturb her, but her husband insisted that I stop in to let her know I was there. For a few hours we talked and laughed, and she invited me to sit on the bed. She taught me something that night that I will never forget: "Amen" means "and so be it."

I was amazed that when she had the opportunity to complain, she decided not to. Instead she decided to teach and share good thoughts. After we finished talking, I walked to the guest waiting area. During the night, I thought about how precious time is and how important it is to make the best of it. This life is not a rehearsal; the time to take action is now. This one life comes with one death, and it takes with it all of our *shoulda's*, *coulda's*, and *woulda's*.

After Mrs. Cunningham was released, I would ride to her house during my lunch break and sit outside in my car for thirty minutes to an hour in silence. I informed her and her husband that if they came out and I was there to please ignore me and continue with their regular routine. I was not there to visit; I was there to sacrifice my time for the healing of her cancer. One day she insisted that I come in. She wanted to thank me for sacrificing my time for her. While taking my seat I noticed books everywhere. The smell of fresh plants and the meticulous placement of the furniture reminded of how the presence of a sweet woman can turn a house into a home. While giggling over deli sandwiches and homemade potato chips, we exchanged our thoughts on books that we were reading and the importance of being grateful for the only life that you will ever have.

She became comfortable enough with me to tell me that she was afraid. Mrs. Cunningham was a short woman with a big presence. She was smart and confident. I took notice of her freshly painted red nails as she turned the pages of a book she had recently read. She politely put the book down and reclined back into the sofa. "Toke, I did not realize that I was this sick," she said as she clutched her hands together. I braced myself for her next words. "I have been sick before, but never like this." Somehow, in my heart, I knew what she was saying. I sat silently for a moment, not really sure how to respond. I couldn't imagine what she was going through. "Mrs. Cunningham, I am here to do whatever you need me to do. I can sit outside in my car a whole week if it would make you feel better." I said with warm eyes. She could feel death closing in on her. Every time I looked at her, I had to hold back my anger because I had death's attention and I wanted to shout "Leave her alone!" She continued to talk and share her fears. I couldn't understand what she saw knowing that she was going to die in a little while. What happens to the heart when you have a beautiful, healthy family; a wonderful home; good friends; and you are still going to die in a little while? I don't know the answer, but I do know that life looks different when it's you. Life looks different when the disease is swimming through your blood, and when the doggone weirdness has set up camp in your body.

Patricia Cunningham died in 2004. A few months before she died she wrote me a letter. When I first read it, I was appreciative of her warm gesture and her kind words. I could feel the sincerity in her heart. Now that I was living with a disease, I re-read her letter and understood how much my sacrifice meant to her. I am glad that I chose to sacrifice my time. Now that the tables had turned, I knew what she felt when she looked out her window and saw me in my car sacrificing my time for her speedy recovery. I now know what it feels like when kindness hugs you back; when it warms your heart, promising you that everything is going to be all right.

The day will come when the strength of your spirit will become stronger than your thoughts. There have been days when I could feel my positive thoughts sliding right off of my brain. Then my spirit stepped up to the plate to complete the job, and the job was to carry this soul when it cannot carry itself. When I was not well, it seemed as if every act of kindness came right on time. I was carried through by the words of encouragement, the flowers, the warm get-well cards, and those individuals who rearranged their schedule to fit mine. All of a sudden I was walking in Patricia Cunningham's shoes, and I was glad because I needed some of her appreciation for life to help me move forward. Once upon a time, I was her strength; now her will to live was my strength. It is true, "What goes around comes back around." The good that you put out is the good you will get back. It is a rich investment because you never know when you're going to need it. The words of encouragement that I had given her, I now had to give myself. Kindness is truly something you can't give away because it makes its way back to you.

I dressed Mrs. Cunningham's hair for the funeral. She was my first and last deceased customer. In her letter, she referred to me as her angel. When I finished dressing her hair, I whispered in her ear, "If you considered me your angel, I hope that I have led you in the right direction. Thank you, Mrs. Pat." I had no idea what I was thanking her for until now. We have all benefited from someone else's labor. I know now that I was thanking her for not giving up. I was thanking her for fighting for her life. When I was losing my vision, I walked in her footsteps and fought. I cannot physically see all of the people who were here on this earth before me, but I know for sure there had to be some winners and some fighters, and Patricia Cunningham was one of them.

She is my soul friend, a person who I met without reason and the result of it was everlasting good for my soul. This would be the person in the grocery line scrambling around in their pockets to help you pay your tab, or someone who pulls over on the side of the road to ensure you have the help you need. I do not know the names of most of my soul friends or even remember all the details about our encounters. The one thing my soul remembers is that it was not in their plans to harm me. The effect of meeting a soul friend is for eternity: A moment in time that stretches into years. When life frightens you, sometimes a good memory or a positive reflection is the best form of healing.

I believe we all want to make a difference. I've heard it said that to the world you might be one person, but to one person you might be the world. Patricia Cunningham made me feel as though I was that one person for her, and I was humbled to be that person in her life. No matter how much she said I influenced her life, I know she influenced mine more. She was my angel. Our greatest gifts live inside of our biggest obstacles, but you can only see this if you're looking for it!

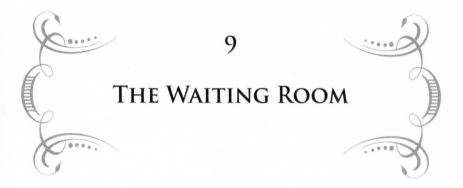

9

THE WAITING ROOM

*"One moment of patience may ward off great disaster.
One moment of impatience may ruin a whole life."*
—*Chinese Proverb*

Patience is a virtue. I heard this quite often growing up in an environment where the elders' words—the cooks, the dishwashers, the maids, and the Sunday school teachers—were believed more than Harvard scholars and presidents. Even facts didn't stand a chance against these pillars of the community. One lady in particular jogs my memory. I can't remember her name, so I'll call her Ms. Emma Jean Hadley. She was an advocate for righteousness. If you did not know what was right, she would be the one to teach you. Yep, that's right. You didn't even have to ask for her opinion; it was in your face before it could register in your mind.

One hot summer day, a group of us kids were walking up the hill when we saw Ms. Emma Jean Hadley coming down the hill. Even now I can feel the fire in my pants. Our hearts stopped, and we looked at each other as if we had seen a ghost. "Ooh, here comes Ms. Emma Jean Hadley," we said in unison. Then we took a moment to breathe because her presence alone could take the breath out of you. We were so afraid of her. Before she could get close enough to hear us, we recited her motto in a sing-song manner, "Patience is a virtue."

In those days, older people used their hands to help you understand something you had not learned even after surviving the previous consequences for breaking their laws. If they told you to sit down and you kept moving, suddenly you might feel a pinch on the leg that felt like your flesh was being twisted by a pair of pliers. Or if they called your name and you kept talking, in about two seconds they'd pull your ear. It felt like your eardrum was going to slide right out of your head. When Ms. Emma Jean Hadley wanted to ensure that you understood what she was saying so you wouldn't forget, she would squeeze the dickens out of your wrist. These little ladies looked harmless, but they were strong.

One day I thought I had hit the jackpot. I was fortunate enough to save what felt like a pound of pennies. I had a habit of counting my coins. The heavier they felt in my pocket, the more I would count them. After I had counted them five times while standing in my front yard, I felt I was being watched. I don't know where she came from, but Ms. Emma Jean Hadley was standing right there. Before I knew it, she had positioned her hand around my wrist. I could feel her preachy intent as she struggled to get a good grip.

"Settle down young lady and be patient!" she said. "I know that thirty-nine cents is about to burn a hole in your pocket. Ya rushin' nowhere and don't even know it. Patience is a virtue. Now act like somebody told you about it."

After she let go of my wrist, I was sure I'd need my thirty-nine cents to buy a box of ace bandages for my wrist. Kids have a great memory, especially when you tell them something over and over again, which these pillars in the community had a habit of doing when they witnessed you breaking their laws. I am mighty grateful for the "Emma Jeans" of my youth who had enough conviction to tell me something that stuck.

However, there is one thing I have definitely learned with age. Even though patience, which is simply the act of waiting, can save our lives, it is the last thing we want to do. There is even something to be learned while waiting in a waiting room. The place is not relevant. It can be the principal's office, a restaurant, a car dealership, a bank, or the doctor's office. You even have to wait to die. The lesson to be learned is "wait your turn." Waiting has taught me patience, and to my surprise, it taught me about forgiveness. If you are patient long enough, you will make the same mistakes you have criticized others for making.

My life experiences have shown me that what I think is going to happen while I'm waiting is usually different from what actually happens. No matter the results, if you are able to leave the waiting room, you still have a chance. Life is not over in the waiting room; it is simply changing. It wanted to change long ago, but you wouldn't let it. A few years ago, I asked one of my mentors, "If you could tell me one thing what would it be?"

Her response was, "Don't be in a hurry for anything, be patient."

For an entrepreneur, patience is mental suicide. This wasn't the advice I was looking for. However, this bit of advice appeared in my life over and over again. Eventually I figured out that even though I was in a hurry, life was not. I have found that I do not need to agree with wise thoughts before they take hold in my life. One day they show up and they are stronger and smarter than your instinct. News flash to all leaders and entrepreneurs: Yes, it is true. One day you will need more than instinct to survive. It may get you started and keep you going, but only wisdom can keep you sane. Maybe my mentor said this because she knew that if I lived a little longer, I would be sitting in life's waiting room.

One night I nearly had a nervous breakdown while waiting on test results that would determine if I had leukemia. I wasn't nervous when I took the test, and even a few weeks after that I was still calm. But the night before my doctor was going to tell me the results, all my doubt had gathered in my chest. I could feel the tiptoeing steps of anxiety pacing around my back. Why was I feeling so wretched? I had taken tests before: a pregnancy test, an AIDS test, and a drug test. But this was a test that would determine whether I had an illness that might eventually kill me. What was the big deal? What was all the internal fuss about? Life had let me live long enough to see innocent and good-hearted people die. The ones who always forgave others; the ones who fed others and fought for others. You know the ones!

It did not help that I had all of the symptoms associated with leukemia. I remember that morning sitting in my house thinking of someone to call. At the time I was alone, waiting for a friend to come and pick me up and take me to my doctor's appointment. As it got closer to my appointment time, the inside of my stomach began to boil from those darn insecurities. I just wanted to hear the voice of someone other than the big-mouth shouting inside of my head. So I called my mentor.

"Well, good morning there, Ms. Webb. How are you?"

"Oh, I'm fine. How are you?" I asked as the tears filled my eyes. I just could not believe that I was going through something so unexpected and so deathly painful. My feelings were hurt.

"So this morning your doctor will share with you the results from your leukemia test." It was not a question, but a conversation starter.

"Yes, ma'am. Today is the day." My heavy tears soaked the top part of my blouse as I conjured up a lie. "Oh, I feel confident that the test will be negative." I was too scared to be honest.

"You know it's okay to be scared, and rightly so considering that you have been through so much these last few months," she said soothingly.

"Yes, I know, but I have to think positive," I said. "Do you remember a phone conversation we had one evening while I was preparing to leave the barbershop a couple of weeks ago?"

"I think so."

"I said to you that my life is growing so fast that when I finally learn something, it's time to learn all over again?"

"Yes, I remember that conversation," she said in a kind of motherly where-are-you-going-with-this tone.

"I'm saying all of that to say that I don't have time to be scared. I must continue to think positive," I explained, more to remind myself than her.

"Being human doesn't mean that you are not being positive, Ms. Toke. It means that you are being honest with yourself," she said gently.

I was grateful to hear such simple, honest advice before I stepped out the front door. What I did not tell her was my self-doubt had punked me out, and I felt as if the whole world was watching me. My concern was that people would somehow be able to look into my heart and see all the tears that I had shed the night before. If the test was positive, I did not want to have to deliver the bad news to my mother. I could not bear breaking my mother's heart in any kind of way, even if I wasn't in control of the situation. Mothers by nature are warm, strong, and caring, especially when it concerns their children. No mother wants her child to become deathly ill before her; no mother wants her child to die before her. This kind of news alone might be too much, even for the strongest mother to bear.

I had no idea that so many thoughts could develop in my head while I waited on test results. For instance, I can't count the number of people who told me to just pray about it. My immediate thought was to ask if they would like to trade eyes with me. My second thought was to wonder exactly what they thought I'd been doing all these years when the heat in my eyes caused the inside of my ears to roast. I sure wasn't tap dancing on the ceiling. The results of the test would alter my future plans and force me to make more room in my life for something else that caused me pain. If this disease was worse than the wait, I would surely die.

Waiting on the doctor to render his findings, his thoughts, and his verdict was insufferable. And worse, I was waiting on him to decide what would be best for my health when I've been eating healthfully, exercising regularly, praying, and treating people the way that I wanted to be treated. Wasn't I already doing what was in my best interest? So what was all that for when the test still might come back positive? When I finished speaking with my mentor, I tried my best to think positive. But my mind would not stop thinking realistically, and time was winding down. The person who was scheduled to drive me to the doctor was due to arrive at any moment. While I still had a few minutes before I left, I sat in silence. The shock of all that was happening left me speechless because I never saw it coming.

For some reason I thought about something the actor Gregory Peck said in his biography: "It is too late to turn back now." I had made up in my mind that whatever was waiting for me at the doctor's office had been there all along. Whether the test was positive or negative was out of my control. Suddenly the feeling of total peace suffused my mind, body, and soul. When you realize that you can't stop the rain, you stop worrying about things that are out of your control. If you really want to face the truth, the only thing that we have control over is our response to the monkey on our back.

I have also come to the conclusion that my journey is always a step ahead of me. My situation may be new to me, but it is not new to my journey. I must admit that I wish my journey would have given me the heads up on this one. Who would have ever thought that one could experience so much internal drama waiting on test results? This experience alone forever changed how I viewed some-one when they were waiting on test results, regardless of what it was for: their physical, breast cancer, or HIV/AIDS. I now understand how my soul friend Patricia Cunningham felt when she confided to me that she was afraid to see her doctor because he was going to tell her if her cancer had returned. Now that I had experienced this firsthand, I understood the expression on her face while she waited in her car at the barbershop one warm afternoon. For years I could not put into words her facial expression as I walked up to her car to see what the problem was. Now I know that fear had pushed her nerves through her face. She was frightened. Apparently her previous bout with cancer had made it evident that one trip to the doctor can change the entire course of your life. I am sure that she found herself saying, "After all, it's too late to turn back now."

Waiting on test results taught me that you can go to sleep in your own shoes and wake up in someone else's. Overnight you can become the person you unconsciously criticized and that person's face will be a reminder to be careful of even the subtle thoughts of criticism that come to mind.

As I arrived at the doctor's office, I felt so limp, as if there were nothing on the inside of my body but air and veins. Immediately I began to think back to the previous visits to doctors and emergency rooms. Different faces appeared in my mind of people that I did not even know I remembered. I could see the faces of the people who were in a rush or irritable (mad at the world, or so I thought). Then there were those people who seemed extremely patient, slow to move, and slow to speak. I had assumed that the person who was rushing was not only irritable, but rude and obnoxious. However, waiting with people who are terminally ill has taught me otherwise. When you get devastating news from the doctor, the first thought usually is to tell someone you love. The person that I had considered to be rude and obnoxious could have been the person who had just received a call from his wife: "Honey, she is only three years old. The doctor said it has settled in her brain the way ants settle in dirt. We are lucky if she lives a week."

A while back, when I was waiting on the nurse to come into the room, my sister called. I am sure she could sense the fear in my voice because before we could even start our conversation, she asked, "Which doctor are you seeing today?" And then before I could respond, she said, "I'll be right there." Now when I see someone who appears to be impatient, I remember my sister and the importance of restructuring my unconscious negative thoughts, especially when they pertain to innocent people. Waiting on test results has a way of making you reflect on the past. I think some of the mind rambling comes from the search within to see if you have committed a crime that was so harsh that you deserve to suffer. Then comes the reality that no one is exempt.

Waiting on the test results also made me aware of all the insecurities that lived inside of my mound of confidence. Yes, confidence and insecurities can live in the same place. Confidence is just taller! I pictured in my mind what life would look like if I had leukemia and if I didn't have it. There was one thing I saw in both pictures—that happiness is a choice. I saw my insecurities as opportunities to look at things from a different perspective.

When the doctor came through the door, I could feel my bowels swimming around inside the walls of my belly. Anybody who has ever gone through this situation knows that if you're not religious, you will be for the next ten minutes. My doctor was so calm as he walked past me to retrieve my test results from his computer. I thought, *No doctor wants to give their patient bad news.* As he swiveled around in his chair, I kept my eyes on the printout of the results in his hand.

He calmly said, "Chitoka, I don't know what to tell you. We have tested you for everything that could be associated with this eye disease. They have all come back negative, and your leukemia test is negative too."

I leaned over and said, "I know what you can tell me, 'Chitoka, get up now and go to the bathroom.' " As the door closed behind me, I heard him laughing.

However, after three years of trying to figure out what disease was plaguing me, my doctor finally diagnosed me with a chronic autoimmune blood disease called Behcet's. It can cause life-threatening problems, and the disease usually afflicts men and women in their 20s and 30s. Often called the Silk Road disease, referring to the old silk route that spans the region from Japan and China in the Far East to the Mediterranean Sea, Behcet's disease is most common in the Middle East, Asia, and Japan. It is extremely rare in the United States. This of course made me wonder how in the heavens did it find its way to Nashville, Tennessee?

Behcet's disease inflamed my eyes and in turn that inflammation caused my uvula tract (the tunnel we see through) to swell and close. This caused my pupil, iris, and retina to stick together. When they unstuck themselves, a greasy film covered my eyes. As this cycle repeated during flare-ups, the film hardened and thickened. Neither Behcet's disease nor the Panuveitis is considered genetic or to be associated with lifestyle choices, occupational history, geographical location, or environmental factors.

Waiting to hear about a test result like this is a moment that I wish I could have avoided. Then one day I found myself telling my story to a stranger. And when asked what I'd have done differently, I immediately responded, "I know now there was no need to do anything different. It was one of the most difficult times of my life, but I would not have traded it for anything." I knew in my heart that whatever emotion I might experience, it wasn't new. The world is made up of people who all enter one way and exit one way. Now, where some of us go after we exit is a different story, I guess! However, we all experience the same thing in different ways, with different eyes, and for different reasons.

I love aging because it has proven that I was wrong about a lot of things, and to be honest, I don't think I could have been convinced any other way. My adolescent mind could not have fully understood the phrase, "There is nothing new under the sun." This is something I heard when I was young and learned when I was older. One day I just woke up and understood. Of course I never knew when I was younger that I didn't quite understand what it meant. Like everyone else, I had to experience something first before I understood what my grandfather said umpteen years ago. Then I had to admit that it was not that his brain had developed Alzheimer's just yet. It was that my brain had not quite developed. Before I knew it, I wanted to run up to him and tell him that he was right, but it was too late. He had been dead for six years now.

Age has helped me look back over my life to see what I've missed. I want to remember the look on my face when I thought that I was right, now that I know I was completely wrong. Visits to my grand-parents' home were often the most puzzling. My grandfather had this particular chair that only he could sit in, and my grandmother made coffee every morning at the same time. This routine followed them into old age. As a child, I could not understand sitting in the same chair forever or making a pot of coffee every two hours. The chair is one of my earliest memories of my grandfather. To me, the chair had been around forever. I wondered what would happen to the chair if he died. I wondered if they had caskets for chairs that only your grandfather can sit in. At the funeral, would they just sit him in the chair?

As I stretched my mind, I never imagined that with age I would develop my own strange quirks that puzzle even me. I can't pinpoint when I developed these quirks. They just happened one day, and it infuriated me to no end. One of my quirks that bullies me around is my need for neat, precise, razor-edge creases. More than one crease in my clothing unnerves me to the point where I feel like something is crawling on me. I am ashamed to say that I have picked up clothes from the cleaners that had double creases and put them directly into the trash, along with the plastic and the receipt. On one occasion I had just purchased a pair of pants that would complement a blouse I was going to wear over the weekend. When I picked them up from the cleaners, I saw a second crease that probably only I would see. But I saw it! I knew my only option was to trash the tragedy, even though I had looked forward to wearing them over the weekend. After I sat in my car for thirty minutes, I came up with a solution. I would ask the lady at the cleaners to wash out the crease and start over. As always she agreed. Once they were dry cleaned again, I could still see the second crease slightly. Needless to say, as soon as I left, I put them in the trash.

One evening while trashing double-creased clothing, I thought to myself, "I might be better off finding a favorite chair to sit in. This is an expensive quirk."

One Sunday morning in 2005, while I was preparing myself for the day, I learned something about myself that deepened my appreciation for the small things in life. At the time, my vision was extremely poor and to make matters worse, I had refused all invitations for a part-time or full-time live-in companion. I did not want to live with someone I could not see, so I learned how to take care of myself with my limited vision. I wore sunglasses inside the house because the light shining in through the windows felt like needles poking me in my eyes. The darkness from the glasses ate up the glare and the halos hanging around the microwave, television, doorknobs, and light fixtures. This made it easier to make things out once I got close enough to feel the objects. I'd feel the furniture to determine exactly where I was in the house or how close I was to the front door. To get from the front of the house to the back of the house, I'd feel the walls. I thought I was managing fairly well, and I assumed I had everything under control.

While preparing myself for the day, I decided that I was going to iron a pair of pants. My attire for the evening was a black business suit. The color black was the most challenging for me to see, feel, and identify because it looked like a black hole. If something was the color black, I had to feel the fabric to determine its identity. I never would have imagined the power a pair of pants could have when my quirks had a strong hold over my mind. As I was about to start ironing, I searched for the crease. My fingers walked around inside the pants and I felt what I thought were two creases.

Well, I knew I had to be feeling the wrong thing because I was looking for one crease, not two. I thought to myself, "Maybe it's all in my mind." I switched to the other pant leg almost in a state of panic, hoping to resolve this big old mess. As I felt around, I heard the sound of my heart racing in my ears. Surprisingly, at my fingertips were three creases, not just two. Were they multiplying on me? As this began to register, I could feel the blood rushing through the veins in my wrists.

I cannot put into words what I felt when I discovered that there were three creases. I took a deep breath and reminded myself that the gentleman who was coming to pick me up would be arriving in forty-five minutes. I put the pants as close to my eyes as I could without poking myself, and the only thing I saw was a blank. I felt the other pant leg only to discover that it also had three creases. This was a catastrophe. I began to sweat, so I sat down for a few minutes to gather my thoughts. By this time my mind was all over the place. *How long had I been wearing a pair of pants that had not two creases but three?* Up until this day I could not have imagined anything worse than losing my vision. There I was on a warm Sunday morning, angry and infuriated at a pair of pants. I decided to give it another shot. My transportation was due to arrive at any time, and answering the door wearing only a blouse and a jacket was not an option.

As I felt the pants again, I searched for the sharpest crease. This only disgusted me more because they all felt the same. I became so agitated that I wanted to put the pants in the garbage disposal and be done with it. I was getting on my own nerves when something came over me. It was a welcoming peace that you get when you battle something and win. I had never felt infuriated about losing my vision. *Why was I in such a mess about three creases? Was this my first indication of what my future was going to be if my vision did not return?* But I had worn those pants countless times and I had never seen more than one crease. I was, of course, almost completely blind.

I started to hate this quirk more than I did losing my vision because I knew if I kept trying, my vision would eventually come back. But how would I deal with this quirk that was there before my eyes started failing me?

My transportation arrived and I answered the door fully clothed. Throughout the day there was a temptation to feel my pants to see if the three creases had mysteriously narrowed to one. My meltdown that morning was an invitation to rethink my battle with this eye disease. After all, these are my eyes, and I am responsible for them whether they are sick or healthy.

I have often wondered where my body and this disease met and became one. Was I sleeping or traveling? Was I praying? When was the date and time? The cycle of life moves without permission. The seasons do change. I believe that hope travels with seasons. That was good news for me and my eyes. I have never been tired enough to give up.

I am often reminded of a phrase that I heard frequently during my barbering career: "You will be fine, just live a little longer." Growing older has helped me look at age from a different perspective. Living longer has offered me the answers to questions that seemed unanswerable when I was younger. Why did my grandfather sit in the same chair for so many years? Why did my grandmother make coffee at the same time for so many years? Was it because with age simplicity becomes attractive? It was evident that my grandparents had their quirks, but age became a gift as they got older. "You will be fine, just live a little longer."

Is it possible to outgrow my dislike for multiple creases? Time will tell. Will I regain all of my sight? Time will tell. What I know for sure is there is nothing new under the sun and life progresses without permission. My grandfather passed away in 2003. We did not bury him with the chair. My grandmother still gets up every morning to make coffee, and I still become slightly agitated when I pick up my clothes from the cleaners and they have two or more creases. Age has taught me that quirks are okay and that they don't define you as a person. They make others aware of certain things that are meaningful to you. Quirks are like seasons in your life. Some things are only for a season and some are for a lifetime. Living a little longer has proven to me that it is all small stuff because whatever the outcome, whether desired or not, the world will continue to rotate.

At the end of the day, I hung up my pants in the closet. I made a decision not to wear them again until I fully regained my vision.

A few months later when I did regain my vision, the first task on my agenda was to investigate my pants. I headed to the closet, determined to get to the bottom of this mystery. To my surprise, my pants did not have three creases; there was only one. My pants had a liner on the inside. Because they were dry cleaned often, the liner had three creases, but the outside of my pants had only one crease. Be patient and learn all the lessons that are waiting for you in the waiting room. You will need them later in life. Don't sweat the small stuff, and it is all small stuff.

10

MY EYES

"No eyes that have seen beauty ever lose their sight."
—*Jean Toomer*

For months I met with my retina specialist. And now, what was in my eyes had spread through my entire body. During one of my visits I became severely ill. The nurses began to whisper among themselves while pointing my way. I felt faint and empty, like I was walking to my grave. The life in me was leaving me there to rot. My eyes were inflamed and the hot blood was sucking my sight away. My body folded like a cushy beach towel. Suddenly I felt a soft hand on my shoulder, followed by a polite command.

"Ms. Webb, why don't you come with me," the nurse said.

My voice was sluggish and my face looked like that of a delusional person.

"Get her a cup of water and meet me in room 109," the nurse said as she so kindly led the way.

"What's been going on with you?" she asked.

Everything seemed to be happening so fast. "I don't know. On my way here I began to feel sick; my whole body got hot and my insides began to feel toasty."

"We need to get you to the ER fast!"

"No, please don't call the ambulance. I can drive myself to Vanderbilt Hospital."

I had been in this situation before, and waiting around for the paramedics to come, strap me down, and ask me the same questions did not seem like much relief.

"But Ms. Webb, you are twenty-three miles away from Nashville," the nurse said. "You need to see a doctor now."

I couldn't hold back. Something inside of me felt like I'd be better off trying to get to the best hospital in the state than going to a doctor in a city that had a population of less than 50,000. I weighed my options and headed for the door. Like I did on the first day I lost my vision, I called my spiritual advisor. My body was smoking hot, and the breeze seeping in through the cracked car windows felt like ice needles.

"Hey, how are you?" I slurred my salutation.

"What's wrong? You sound like you're dying."

I kept my eyes focused on the road while trying to keep the sun from baking the top of my hand on the steering wheel.

"I am on my way to the hospital. I ain't doing too well."

"And you're driving?" I could hear the worry in his labored breathing. "Ms. Toke, you have to stop doing this."

I was already too low to feel bad about my actions. "I know, but I had to leave. I felt like I was dying."

Though I pressed the gas harder, I never went above the speed limit. I arrived at the emergency room just in time. The parking attendant swiftly opened the door, almost choking me to death with his cologne.

"Hello, ma'am," he said. "And who is the patient?"

I thought I might have been better off staying in the other city considering I was the only one in the car. I wanted to scream, "I am, you idiot!" But I could not get it out fast enough. His chest brushed my back as he caught me before I fell to the ground.

"Get me a wheelchair now!" He screamed in a harsh tone.

Within seconds, it felt like a body was lying on top of me, but it was several heavy-duty hospital blankets. My temperature was over 102 degrees, and I was freezing. The next voice I heard was my spiritual advisor praying in my ear, assuring me that everything was going to be alright.

"I am cold," I managed to say. "I need another blanket."

"Chitoka, this is Dr. Hammon," the doctor said. "We're going to starting running tests to see if we can find what's causing your temperature to rise. The first test will be a spinal tap."

I had to use all of my energy to sit up straight for this test.

"If you feel a warm secretion running down your back, it's okay. We'll clean it up." The doctor rested his cool hands on my shoulder.

It was uncomfortable for a while, but once the test was over I could lie back down. The night went by slowly. As I went in and out of consciousness, I could see my mother flicking the television station back and forth looking for the local news station. She had her Bible in her right hand and the remote in her left hand. As the morning began to make its presence known, the sun coming in through the large window warmed the blanket on top of my stomach. I could hear what sounded like troops coming toward my door. An older man in a pressed white lab coat walked into my room.

"Good morning, Chitoka, my name is Dr. John Sergent, and I'm going to be your doctor from now on."

I looked up at him like he was God, hoping he had Jesus' magic touch when he turned two fish into enough food to feed 5,000 people. He then placed his hand on top of my hand. This reassured me that I had the right doctor in my corner. His hand was as warm as his introduction. Before he left he asked me if there was anything that I would like to tell him.

"Yes," I said. "Thank you and I appreciate your help."

He then leaned down and said, "Don't worry. I'm going to take care of you." During the two years of tests, he never wavered from taking excellent care of me.

Oh! How I wish I had been a child when this disease and my life became one. I'm certain that I wouldn't have toiled daily with the thought of this ravaging beast of a disease leaving me disabled. Children do not keep a list of their symptoms. Instead they like to help mommy make the grocery list and write and rewrite their Christmas list throughout the year. Children don't keep track of the disease's presence or play the "pity me drum roll." They don't ask, "What did I do to deserve this?" Children don't concern themselves with things that are out of their control. As a matter of fact, they think they control everything. Maybe that's why sometimes they often respond to adults' questions by asking their own questions. Unlike adults, children don't try to hide their pain and emotions. If it hurts, they tell you it hurts. If it stinks, they tell you it stinks. I call this innocent confidence: Once it enters the mind, it flows right out of the mouth. All they know is when they feel bad, they want to feel better.

In the past, I had worried myself sick because the statistics showed that I would most likely suffer a lot because I've had just about every symptom of Behcet's disease. But I can tell you that if Behcet's disease was looking for a fighter, it met its match. If I don't know nothing else, I do know that fighting back increases your chances of winning, and learning how to lose guarantees your chance of winning.

I took my eyes for granted. My eyes had always been good to

me, and because of my assumptions I never had an eye exam. When my eyes turned on me, I realized that they had a say-so, and it was a force to be reckoned with. I wanted my eyes back on the team; we had been friends for twenty-nine years. There were moments when I wished I had the ability to look into my own eyes and say, "What in the world are you doing to us?" I wanted my eyes to do what they had done all of my life: Show me who I am and allow me to see what was in front of me. In other words, I wanted my eyes to show me if my socks complemented my shoes or if someone's facial tick means that they've lied to me.

Your eyes will force you to understand that you will only see what you have the ability to understand. Yes, time is the main ingredient that brings everything to light; time will make you grateful for every organ that works in your body, including your skin. When your body separates from its healthy state, it is separating from you. This feels like you're in the middle of the ocean and your safety jacket is floating away. As it floats farther and farther away, you become so frightened that something else kicks in. You don't fight it; you willingly take a back seat and surrender. Before you know it, you are standing on solid ground. Just as amazed are the people standing before you who think you were strong and determined and that's why you weren't defeated. Maybe you even possess some supernatural powers. When in reality, you were not this big ball of strength. You just knew when to let go.

Hope transforms into survival when you let go of something you can't handle. Your only hope is what is stored in your mind. I guess it helps to know some things before you get sick. You will need that hope when good health takes a vacation from your journey. "Way back when" becomes a constant reminder of the good times: the times when I did not have a medication schedule and an expense account for doctor visits, and when sleeping was enjoyable and mornings were always pleasant without the worry of waking up blind. Over the years, I have heard older people say repeatedly that they're thankful they don't have to take medication in the morning. When I was completely healthy, I didn't fully understand how that made it on to the list. Surely there were other things that should have been first. Time is the main ingredient that brings everything to light! Now that I have to gobble down hard powder on a daily basis, I often wish their testimony could be mine. This experience has made me feel powerless.

The inflammation in my eyes made me want to vomit. I was battling two monsters at the same time: heat and pain. During a flare-up, even the medicated eye drops felt like drops of hot sauce. Living with this disease meant where I slept, it slept. Wherever I was, it was present. My mind constantly reminded me that it lives in my eyes and that it will depart on its own terms. My responsibility was to accept its terms. Panuveitis never missed the opportunity to make its presence known through a swollen eye filled with volcanic heat. My vision was one of the many gifts that came in my birthday basket. Now, only twenty-nine years later, here was this disease whose only mission was to destroy that gift.

Some days I was unstoppable; no amount of pain could dampen my hope. Then one thought of going blind would bring me down to the ground. The peace that I felt from meditating was snatched by the fear that waited for me at bedtime. The heart has the ability to crack when your desires are different from what you are experiencing, especially when your ultimate desire is not to experience your current reality. Talk about an emotional twist! I learned through this cycle of life that peace was a state of mind that could not be determined by anyone but me. This gave me the strength to continue to fight for my vision. The more I fought, the more I realized my battle was a mental one not a physical one.

Life seemed stagnant when I thought I had all the answers. It wasn't until I accepted that I did not know the outcome of this moment or what each day would bring that suddenly not knowing felt natural and rewarding. I felt like I could get back to minding my own business and focusing on things I had control over. This was one of my truest experiences with peace. I realized that life had been here longer than I and did not need my help. I needed to save my energy for the days that sapped my strength.

One example of this was when the sun became my enemy. Light from any source—light bulbs, candles, the sun—was equivalent to a double-edged machete. I never imagined light becoming my enemy. While having dinner with friends at an elegant restaurant, the candle on the table would terrorize me with no chance of mercy. Every time I looked at the candle, a sharp razor feeling jolted my eye almost like someone was shooting staples in my eyes with a staple gun. By the time my friends asked that the candle be taken away, the flare-up had already begun, and I just kept my left eye closed for the remainder of the night.

After learning how to live with this illness and accepting its terms, I had to learn how to live when the disease was quiet. I had never realized that there was a whole process to living with an illness. Whew! It is a lot of work, somewhat like working overtime. The stages are (1) being informed you have an illness; (2) testing and blood work; (3) medications; (4) side effects; (5) consultations with your doctors; (6) living with it; (7) checkups; and (8) dealing with all the people who "know somebody who has what you have." This was a full-time job and what my life was like on a daily basis. It is so different from having a cold where you lie around for a few days, eat chicken noodle soup, sweat, and drink enough orange juice for 7.5 million people. And then you are back to your daily routine. When you live with a disease that can kill you, you are going to need more than a glass of orange juice and chicken noodle soup.

The times when the disease was quiet proved to be just as frightening. I felt like it was stalking me, waiting for me to get confident enough to believe I had beaten it. I had longed for the disease to be calm so it did not hurt and I could see clearly. Now I was finally here and anxiety was still my nightly companion, along with enough fear to scare a bowel movement out of a lion. This disease taunted me. The pain was a beast that left me frightened after each episode. So when I wasn't in pain, the thought of the previous episode was enough to paralyze me. Spasms, which felt like a charley horse in my eyes, came as often as I blinked. There were days when attempting to see was not worth it. Once, my eyes were so swollen that my eyelids appeared to be the same size as my lips. My choices were to keep my eyes open and endure the burning and the swelling or to close them for a moment so they could cool off. Sometimes my eyes would burn for so long that I figured eventually my hair was going to catch on fire!

Every flare-up came with the confidence of running its course. It was a total bully; once it set in, it stayed. It came only to destroy. Some days I would fight back, *One day I am going to whip the skin off of you.* On other days I whimpered, *Please don't make it hurt like the last time.* It's true: The same thing that will make you happy will also make you sad. When joy does an about-face, its new identity is pain. I once heard that wherever you find a flower, you find the sun and the rain. This situation made me realize that it is a lot easier to be thankful for a chance that you have rather than the one you've lost. Why did my body have to choose a disease that had the power to destroy it? I wish I had not trusted my eyes so much! Were there no other diseases to choose from? Were there two left and this was the better one?

This sudden turn of events did however confirm that my eyes had other capabilities besides seeing. It was through seeing that I realized that a mind is a terrible thing to waste. Seeing things allowed me to be certain of the things that I had heard, and having an image of something provided me with enough information to determine how it might sound. For example, when you are in your house, you might hear a loud noise in another room. As you race toward the sound, you try to picture what could have fallen. Because the noise was very loud, you know the fallen object was heavy. You try to match the object in your mind with a loud noise. Perhaps it was the microwave or maybe the television fell off the wall. In a sense then, hearing becomes a form of vision. Before you get to the other side of the house, you have figured out what crashed. You were right. The television fell off the wall. Is that why having our five senses is considered to be the ultimate gift?

I can vouch for the fact that if you lose one sense you can find it in another sense; they are all intertwined. At no time during the loss of my vision did I ever feel like I had fully lost my sight, because I learned how to see with my ears. I could hear the sound of a car and tell which direction it was going. I could smell bread and tell whether it was soft or hard. Taste also became another way for me to see. I could taste a cup of coffee and see the freshness shimmering through the air. Hearing someone speak that I had never met before was very telling. Their attitude painted a clear picture of their intent, and sometimes it was not good. Sometimes I felt like my eyes were more valuable than my mind. In my mind I could toss things around and eventually develop a thought. Whatever I saw with my eyes was what it was. There was no tossing anything around and trying to make my mind understand what it saw.

As I traveled between two states to oversee my companies, this disease began to take its toll on me. I could feel my hope dripping away. This was challenging for me because I have always been an optimistic person, and I had overcome so many obstacles. This battle made me look back over my life, hoping to find a reason for this moment. A decline in health of any kind is a wake-up call. It serves as a swift reminder that good health is not automatic or guaranteed but a temporary privilege. It's devastating when your privilege expires.

So I began the long, exhausting search for reasons why bad things happen to good people. With much thought I found one: I am human and I am not exempt from tragedy. Usually the search begins when pain has dominated the mind, broken the heart, and at last reached the soul. For the most part, when the pain has reached the soul the scars are permanent. There is nothing more terrifying than adults who self-diagnosis. Given enough time and a dictionary, we can all come up with a diagnosis.

Self-diagnosing usually comes when we cannot find a reason we want to believe. I could hear my mother's voice when I was a child: "Don't read in the dark. It'll ruin your eyes." "Make sure you eat all of your carrots because they're good for your eyes." Maybe I didn't eat enough carrots. Maybe I should've been honest with my mother about not eating all of my carrots. Maybe that batch I threw in the trash when I was nine would have saved me from this despair. (Of course the beta-carotene from those carrots would not have lasted twenty years!) How many times did I read in the dark with only the light from the television? If only I had turned on all of the lights maybe I would not be facing the hardest time of my life. I was looking for a reason I could believe because my eyes were turning on me.

The disadvantage of having 20/20 vision is the assumption that you will always be able to see clearly.

And not only did *I* want to see—my heart wanted to see, and my mind wanted to see. None of us wanted to live in the dark. I was not the only one that missed my eyes. I had made peace with my soul about going completely blind, just not forever. I am a firm believer in reclaiming what's mine. To seal my peace with blindness, I decided to dive in and fight while bracing myself for whatever came my way.

11

SOMETHING INSIDE OF ME

"Faith isn't faith until it's all you're holding on to."
—Author Unknown

I have always felt the presence of something that loved me as much as I loved myself. I would liken it to the mother who never gives up on children who have lost their way. One hot Saturday evening my mother was driving me and my sisters to the Tennessee State Fair. This was our Disney World because this was all my mother could afford. As she drove, we pushed the ceiling liner, which was hanging down in our faces, back into its place. For whatever reason, the tacks that held it in place were no longer doing the job. My sisters and I also played bingo with every car and person that zoomed by. At times our heads twisted all the way around like we were possessed.

"Bingo! That's my car," my sister said, giggling as if that was really her car.

As we approached the entrance to the fair, a well-dressed lady with a glowing presence entered at the same time. My oldest sister was moving from side to side to avoid being burned by the hot seat of the car. When she saw this woman, she said with a smile, "Whooo! Bingo. That's me." I grinned softly and thought to myself, *Bingo. I want to be like Jesus.* I remember being embarrassed to say this out loud because I didn't want my sisters to make fun of me. I could hear my younger sister saying, "That's not a choice," so I let it ride and kept it to myself.

I did this a lot with experiences that I had with what I call My Something because *It* always seemed bigger than but equal to Jesus. They were one in the same. My inner space has always been occupied by the presence of two energies: me and My Something. Even when I did not know what that something was, I trusted it with my life. What it has given me no human being can match, not even myself. It has given me an understanding that allows me not to confuse simple mistakes with the ways of life. In other words, every bad or unfortunate thing that happens in my life is not the result of some-thing I did wrong. It feels like the natural movement of life that needs no permission to heal, to command, and to take away. It's always on time.

One day while spending the summer at my father's house, my sister was talking on the telephone to some boy she had just met that morning. I could tell he was stealing her heart because her voice got softer, and every time she responded to him she would look at me and wink. I didn't give it much thought because I was mesmerized by the blinking lights on the new see-through phone our father had bought for us the day before. Suddenly I felt a nudge.

"Here," my sister said, extending the phone to me. "It's his friend. He wants to talk to you."

I covered the mouthpiece and said, "Is he ugly?" We both quietly giggled.

"I don't know," she said. "Talk to him and see." We didn't know it then but we were clueless.

"Hey," he said, "what's your name?"

His interest captivated me. "My name is Toke."

I can't remember all the details, but within an hour I was in my car driving to his home. It was after ten o'clock at night, and he lived in a crime-ridden area. I could hear my mother's voice: "Girls should never be out driving anywhere after dark." She'd always say this to me with a pleading look. After I got my first car at sixteen, she reminded me of this daily.

When I arrived at the boy's house, I thought I was home free because even though it was dark, the front area was quiet and there was no one in sight. He had told me his aunt's apartment was on the back side closest to the woods. As I walked toward the stairs to her apartment, it was so quiet I could hear a pin drop. Then I saw two large men standing at the bottom of the steps. I froze and heard my mother's voice again and this time I could see her face.

One of the men came toward me and stepped up onto the first stair. "Who you lookin' for down here?"

I couldn't remember the apartment number, but I did remember the boy's name. "Charles." I knew I didn't have much time. He was coming toward me and I knew they were going to kill me. As my stomached jumped, something inside of me said *he lives in the apartment to the left.*

"I'm looking for Charles," I said. "He lives in that apartment right there." I pointed to the left. They moved aside as if I had been granted a VIP pass. When I got inside, I was so happy that they did not hurt me. I stood in front of the door thinking about what had just happened.

"You're cute," Charles said and laughed.

The poof from his breath burnt my eyes. Now I was really angry with myself for being so stupid. On the ride home I kept saying, "Thank you for being on time."

I have had numerous experiences like this throughout my life, where I was saved by the presence of something inside. It had a tendency to come in the strangest ways, but it always came on time. I soon learned that whether I make the right or wrong decision, these small encounters are coming my way, not to harm me, but to make me stronger. They are unavoidable.

These encounters taught me that if I didn't learn how to think when I was going through them, I would not know what to do when I came out of the situation. I have reflected on my life many times over, and there are so many things that I am extremely grateful for. There is one thing that I've traced back to my birth. Something has been keeping me safe and happy. I can't remember when we met. I just remember it was there before me. It was first. This something used my brain as a note pad. There were always messages of hope and assurance.

Though I couldn't see this something, I felt its presence everywhere. It was in my thoughts, my bones, and my doubts. Wherever I went in life, it was always there first. No matter the situation, it never excused itself. When I was being molested as a child, this something talked to me as the molester finished his course. I listened to My Something as he rubbed my small breast. My Something kept telling me it will be over soon and that I'm still a winner. When I would wake in the morning, there would be messages on my brain. *That was then. This is now, and you're still a winner.*

When I was in the eighth grade, my classmates gave me the best all-around award. I sat in the stands with mixed emotions because although I wanted to win, I did not want to walk across the stage in the outfit my mother had bought me at a yard sale. She had wanted me to be dressed well just in case I won.

The principal announced my name as the winner and raised the award toward the sky. To my amazement as I was walking toward the stage, everyone in the stands stood on their feet and clapped. Before I walked up onto the stage, I could hear My Something saying, *Don't worry about your clothes. You have been a winner all along.*

This something always reminded me, *On the days when I can see you but you can't see me, just remember the notes I left for you.* When I was a teenager I began to put two and two together. This something had been with me all of my life, and it appeared that it was not going anywhere. As I experienced more in life, I began to remember the things that I had heard my mother say over the years. "God will never leave you nor forsake you." I realized what My Something was. My Something was God. When I was losing my vision, I had a conversation with My Something. *It's me. I'm going blind and I'm afraid. By the way, I have payroll to meet on Friday.* The relationship that we had allowed me to share my truest concerns, in any order. Facing new battles did not eliminate the battles that I was currently experiencing. My Something encouraged me to read my worries in the order that they showed up in my life.

It's me. I need you now, I'd keep saying.

Read your notes!

I'm reading my notes. They don't say anything about going blind!

Keep reading!

Aha, "You're still a winner."

My Something always invited me to think past what I perceived as devastating. There were always choices. The choice to do better hung around the way smoke hangs over a barbeque roast. No situation was too complicated for My Something, even the ones that caused me great despair, the ones than ran through my system and reached my soul. When that happened, I did not want to understand and remember my notes. I wanted the "gift" of taking a moment not to care. I assumed that this would be okay every now and then considering that there is only one set of footprints in the sand. When things hurt deeply, there was always a part of my inner self that was healed. So I examined my reaction when I let the hurt take its course. I usually felt that a lesson learned is a lesson that I don't have to repeat. So I learned that some things are supposed to hurt.

Losing my vision was painful. I tried to hold back the fear and disappointment with my mind, but the fear pushed my mind aside. I tried to fight the pain and fear with my heart but they walked over it. Just like that they were ready to take on my soul, but my soul had a partner—My Something. And the buck stops with My Something. I had never had anything taken away from me that was not returned. This was the first time in my life that I could not find my notes.

Yeah! Yeah! I know I'm a winner, but soon I'm going to be a blind winner. I want things to be the way they were before this disease entered my life. I don't want to sleep with worry anymore. I want it out of my bed! How long must I be afraid to blink?

This pit stop along my journey seemed familiar; it appeared to be business as usual. As far back as I can remember there has always been a hill to climb or a mountain to overcome. I must admit, after each mountain that I've climbed, I learned to see the best in me. I guess I just did not expect to still be climbing mountains at twenty-nine. There was a note left on my brain that said, *You didn't expect to still be climbing mountains at twenty-nine. And what exactly do you think you'll be doing fifty years from now?* It was also reassuring to know that no matter how high the mountain was, I would never have to climb it alone. I began to think, *Who are you that you always extend your hand so I can reach the mountaintop? How many more mountains are there? How many do I have to climb to feel whole and complete?* I sat down one evening and wrote a poem to My Something.

Who Are You?

I think of you quite often. I remember you from
way back when.
You showed me your trust at five. I learned to
never doubt you at ten.
Who are you that you are always on, your com-
passion as soft as dew.
You and I both know that I am not perfect, but
is it possible for me to love like you?
My mother was right about you, so were the
older people in the neighborhood.
May I ask where did you get your start? How
does one look at everyone and see good?
Who are you? I have never heard your voice, yet I
hear everything you say.
Your imagination is awesome. What were you
thinking when you created night and day?
Some days I feel like we are one. On other days I
feel like we are worlds apart.
That is okay. Your presence has a long range. I
always feel you hugging my heart.
One last question: Who are you that you make
life clearer and clearer?
One last answer: Who am I? Look in the mirror.

This poem was a reflection of the many emotions that naturally
flow through you when you love like you can't be hurt. I trusted My

Something. I have found that trust is love. It is one of the many ways that you can show your love. It allows you to trust even when you doubt. On the days when you are only strong enough to doubt, it is okay. These are the natural rhythms of love. When I was faced with this illness, sometimes My Something did not answer fast enough. One day I asked, *Is My Something on break?* When I was younger My Something would answer right away. Now that I am older, I think My Something is getting older because the response time is taking longer.

Or maybe it is time for me to start writing my own notes. The time has come for me to participate more fully in my future. The best thing that I can do for myself is to take ownership and responsibility for any and every thing about me, which of course includes the issue with my eyes. After all, My Something did provide me with instructions for the days when It could see me but I could not see It. *Remember your notes!* Aha! Taking ownership and responsibility for your lot in life is what qualifies you as a winner, not the outcome of the situation. This reassured me that my journey is laced with choices that have been here long before my arrival.

Choices are a form of power when you are faced with a situation that offers you no options. You don't always have control of your options, but you always have control of your choices. My Something has always presented me with choices. One note left on my brain was, *The freedom to choose is your invitation to decide.* I was grateful that no matter the outcome, I could choose to continue the life that I was living. I had to learn how to live the same life a different way. Choices! As I have gotten older, there has been one thing that My Something has required of me: *I will make you aware of your choices, but I will not make decisions for you.* As I have reflected on my life during the most challenging times when I was hurting, I assumed that during that time I didn't have a choice—that for whatever reason the choice would just fall from the sky. Wrong! The choice is always mine. My choice is my responsibility. Not when I get ready or when I feel like it, but when it is time to make a choice.

I have lived long enough to know that the opportunity to choose is the DNA for freedom. My Something is not like anything else that I have ever known. It is not even like me. Where we differ is my hope is off and on. My Something's hope is always on. As my vision was deteriorating, my soul was circling around its comfort zone in a panic because we were in unfamiliar territory. I had experienced being under the weather before; however, now I was under the knife. My Something accompanied me through this long period of turbulence: In 2005, I had steroid injections in my eyes to restore my sight; I'd had injections in my legs and arms before but never in my eyes. However, my sight did not fully return until February 2006. In 2007, when my sight deteriorated a second time, I had surgery on my left eye. This was unfamiliar territory and somewhat frightening because the disease always seemed to be one step ahead of my prayers. This was a new place in life for me. All of my past situations came with a glimpse of the outcome. Not this situation. Every day came with its own intricate details. I never could grasp a complete picture.

At eight o'clock in the morning, my eyes would look normal, and six minutes later, they could be swollen like they had been popped in a popcorn machine. The pain of disappointment seeped into my being. Where did this monster come from? I felt vulnerable, and a feeling of defeat was draped across my shoulders. The only thing I had confidence in was My Something. I could trace the tender love back to my birth. Surely My Something wouldn't bring me this far and leave, not this far. For twenty-nine years My Something had been consistent, compassionate, and on time. It had always made my journey worth the fight while revealing to me that okay place within myself. This tunnel within carried happiness and peace to my soul.

According to the older people in the community, there was no other friend like My Something. This was confirmed on the days that I lay in bed going blind second by second. Even during the most trying times in my life, I have never felt like I was all alone. I have always felt the presence of two energies: me and My Something. My hope is that as I get older, I'll continue to get wiser. My Something has taught me that wisdom is smarter than instinct, faster than fear, and stronger than evil. It has taught me that hope is internal before it is external. If you choose to do so, you can find hope in anything around you.

I actually found hope by staring at a clock. It was an old clock that had been in my family for twenty years. It's one of those clocks that you never notice because it is square, a dusty brown color, and had a cord that was long enough to reach from here to Japan. My mother purchased it at a yard sale in the early 80s, and back then, it was already ten years old.

When I was young, I never liked the clock and often wondered why my mother chose the oldest clock at the yard sale. I was never excited about the things that my mother purchased at yard sales. As we moved over the years the clock would always resurface. It was the clock that would not die. There were times when I was tempted to unplug it to see if it would still work properly. It had been dropped and moved around. We surely never resisted the opportunity to use it as a coaster from time to time. Over the years, we had spilled all sorts of beverages on it. Even after dropping and accidentally knocking it off the table several times, amazingly it kept working. Sometimes it appeared that the occasional drops to the floor actually made the clock work even better. No matter what, it would not stop working.

To this day, I am grateful that it did not stop working. Some twenty years later as I was going blind, there by my side was the clock. Of course, as I initially thought about all of the ugly things I had said about it in the past . . . I did not know what a significant role this clock would play in strengthening my confidence. The frightening part for me was not that I was going blind, but that I was going blind slowly. Every day would get a little bit darker and a little bit darker. But one day to my surprise, I awoke to find the numbers on the clock to be a bright, bursting red. I knew then that if I could see the digital clock I still had a chance.

So I positioned the clock about six feet from where I was sleeping. If I could see the clock from this distance and the numbers remained clear, this would be my indicator that even though my vision was deteriorating I could still see enough to live a normal life. So every morning I would pop my eyes open to make sure I could still see. Then I would look directly at the clock. Measuring how well I could see the clock gave me hope. Before I went to sleep, I would say to the clock, "I want to see you in the morning." Some mornings I would awake and the numbers were a red blur that looked like a flashlight. On those days I would tell the clock, "If we're going to work as a team, I need you to do your part." Of course the clock did not respond. In the beginning, I was thankful that I could barely see the red numbers on the clock. As my vision decreased, I became thankful for the blur. The last thing I would do at night before I closed my eyes was look at the clock. Seeing the clock was an accomplishment for me.

On one of my many visits to my retina specialist, he confirmed that my disease was not stable. This was devastating news, and I thought silently to myself, *But I can still see the clock.* This helped me see how the disease would sneak up on me. In my mind if I could see the clock, I could see enough not to feel doomed. It can be frustrating attempting to monitor a disease that has no gauge. On most occasions, I did not know if my eyes were going to run hot because there were no warning signs that the boiling sensation was right around the corner. Many people have asked me if losing my vision just happened one day. The first response that came to mind was, "If you live a little longer you'll come to understand that no person alive is exempt from anything."

I once heard in a song that "you have to have faith to have understanding." I now translate that to mean that you must believe in yourself to understand all the great things that live within you. I am okay with my lot in life even though this disease has taken me on a detour that wasn't on my map. But this is my journey, and I am responsible for this beautiful gift. Age, circumstances, and love for other people have a way of making me appreciate my lot in life regardless of the boulders that roll through with the intent of knocking me flat on my face.

The clock was a form of inspiration, and it allowed me to release the expectations I had stored in my mind. I knew I could be inspired by a book or normal daily events. However, I never thought I could be inspired by an old, dusty brown clock that piqued my mother's interest some twenty years ago at a yard sale. The clock convinced me that an open mind does not allow you to decide how you will be inspired. When I would return home, I would give the clock an update of my doctor's visit. I wanted to confirm that we were of one accord. I was convinced that the clock was my plastic friend. It certainly gave me the space I needed to hope and believe, the way friends make themselves available when you are in need of a shoulder to cry on. My heart smiled, because now I was learning to write my own notes.

12

WE HAVE ALL BENEFITED FROM SOMEONE ELSE'S LABOR

"When we seek to discover the best in others,
we somehow bring out the best in ourselves."
—*William Arthur Ward*

As human beings age, a past is created. In spite of what you see a person to be today, we all come with a past. Every second contains a piece of history, and if you listen to the stories of your elders, you will be able to visualize the movement of history. It is the connection between now and then. My most favorite thing to do as a child, and still do today, was to sit and talk with my elders. The older they were, the more mesmerized I was. Being in their company afforded me the privilege, in some cases, to have the answers of life before the test. I considered their wisdom as my cheat sheet to life.

The older they were, the more convinced I was. One of the most valuable lessons they taught me was time waits for no one. So you need to be all you can be with the time you do have. Contrary to what many people believe, time does run out. Time does not run out of time; we run out of time.

We are all filled with moments in time. Like these moments we eventually pass. But unlike these moments we leave this atmosphere. These precious moments that taught me lessons were here long before I was born. They will be here long after I am gone, waiting patiently to teach someone else. I have learned not to fight these moments. This is their domain, and they are wiser than thought and longer than life. Understanding how people in the past dealt with unfavorable moments encouraged me. What I found to be consistent with people who overcame moments that seemed like a lifetime is they all got tired.

Being tired of a situation has a way of making you aware of your self-worth. It also serves as a reminder that you have other options. Usually when you become tired of a situation, you can't live with it anymore. So you're reminded that your other option is death, which makes the situation seem doable. Being tired of a situation is the beginning of waking up—waking up to the million other possibilities that live in the same moment as the tragedy. I soon realized that going blind was not the end of the world; death was the end of the world.

Your soul shouts: *It's too soon to quit!* But you protest that it can't be done. *Either we get out now or we die later.* But your soul says, *Yes you can.* It feels like your soul is turning, and as it is turning, it is standing, and as it is standing, it begins to speak powerfully. *We are all related to chance.* It is the opportunity to get up and do something different, make a way out of no way, turn a nickel into $1.15, turn a meal for one into a meal for seven.

One morning I woke up and heard Stevie Wonder being interviewed on the television. The reporter asked him how he felt about going blind as a child. His response was: "I didn't feel bad. The kid in the next room at the hospital died." When your choice is death or blindness, you don't need to be a rocket scientist to make the decision. Stevie Wonder's bright smile on the television always lights up the room. With every step I take, he reminds me that even though I can't see the footprints on the ground of the people who lived before me, they are there. And there are many. I have chosen to follow in the footprints of my elders.

After all, I can hear My Something telling me, *When you come to a crossroad in life consider your elders.* How the people of the past generation made it through trials and tribulations is a fail-safe method for my generation. Get tired, get up, and get going! What I know about business I learned from my elders, most of whom I don't know personally. I learned from my elders that you reap what you sow and that you should strive to treat people right. Following in the footsteps of my elders gave me a mature attitude imbued with excellence, integrity, and responsibility. My motto for my businesses is, "We treat people the way we want to be treated." Life is not designed for us to reinvent the wheel. It is designed for us to spin the wheel when it's our turn. We have all benefited from someone else's labor. Now it is important that I live my life in such a way that someone can learn from my experience. I am now responsible for guiding someone else's steps because so many other people were responsible for guiding mine. These are the moments that make us equal because no matter who you are or where you reside, we are all walking in someone else's footprints. They are there with or without your permission, waiting for you to step in, because if you don't the tracks will disappear.

I can assure you that life does take detours. When that time comes, it's a relief when you realize you don't have to figure out this maze called life, but that you're included in a group of people who live their lives responsibly and fairly. With this being the goal, it was important for me to understand that everything I did affected other people. As my eyesight deteriorated, I thought of all the people who would benefit from my strength and courage. It's easier to fight when I realize I am fighting for the team. Every time Martin Luther King Jr. got up to speak out against injustice, he was speaking for the team. Every time Princess Diana spoke out against child poverty, she was speaking for the team. Every time Bono sings to the world about AIDS awareness, he is singing for the team. We are all apart of one team.

If you want to understand something, try to change it. I am sure that every time someone spit in Martin Luther King's face, he realized the power of prejudice and the limitations of all human beings. We have the ability to be severely cruel and the choice to unashamedly love. In my experience, I have found that people who are cruel to others have one thing in common: They might voice a strong dislike for one particular thing, but at the end of the day, no one is exempt from their cruelty. There is an enormous amount of love within a person when you can withstand someone calling you names and spitting in your face while your only crime is having been born. As the megaphones busted King's eardrums with derogatory remarks and as the hot spit rolled down his face, his only response was, "We shall overcome."

I want to love like that. If I don't benefit from his labor, his walk would have been in vain. My soul knows it is cruel and unjust to hold an entire race accountable for the heinous acts of a few people. If that was the structure of our justice system, every race alive would be found guilty of something. Fortunately love is stronger than evil. Evil has the ability to run rampant when people focus on their beliefs more than their actions. When I put all of my energy into awakening my consciousness to my actions, I join a universal love that flows without permission. It is like jumping on a roller coaster that is already rolling.

Treating people the way that I want to be treated is always in the front of my mind because I know the roller coaster comes back around and delivers what you loaded onto it. Hmm! Right ain't never wronged nobody! I learned from Patricia Cunningham that what you do to others, you do to yourself. I noticed that what I did for her, someone else did for me during my illness. Now when I read her letter, I am reminded that you can only escape death for so long. As I get older, I accept that dying is a beautiful part of living. Death is evidence that time is my most precious and valuable asset. It is a gift from an entity that sees everyone as deserving of this gift that you cannot give away. I know if I waste time, I am not being a good steward of this gift. Not forgiving people is the biggest time waster because forgiveness keeps love flowing. This also includes forgiving yourself.

When Mrs. Cunningham died, I was hurt because I wanted her to live; I had a few more words to say. I soon realized I was being selfish because perhaps she was ready to die. What if she didn't have anything else to say? When I read her letter, I could hear death in the background.

November 7, 2003
Dear Toke,

I would like to thank you for all you have done during my illness. The time you share with me is a great blessing for my physical healing, my spirit, and my soul.

I continue to remember how you have ministered and prayed with me for my recovery. I appreciate all the time you share with me and all the special acts of kindness you do for me.

You are my angel and I thank God for you, for you have been truly a blessing to me and my family.

I truly believe that prayer changes things and that "The prayers of the Righteous Availeth Much." My life and healing is a testimony to the power of God.

I pray God's blessings for you and your ministry. If I can ever do anything for you, do not hesitate to call upon me. Keep me in your prayers.

With gratitude and love,
Patricia Cunningham

When I first read her letter I was taken back by her referring to me as her angel. I considered this to be the highest compliment that a human being could give to someone. Never again will I allow myself to believe that my prayers don't mean anything. I will not allow myself to believe that my vote doesn't count. Once while I was watching the *Oprah Winfrey Show* Bettie Hooker, the guest, told Oprah that we should "always say kind things to people because you may not remember as the years pass, but they will." I am certain that Mrs. Cunningham thought she was the only recipient of the kindness that was flowing between us. Little did she know that a few years later I would develop a disease that would threaten my sight, and that my strength would derive from her courage.

On the days when I get tired of this disease that will not leave on demand and it is so stubborn that even medication can not make it leave, I read her letter. It is my reminder that eventually you reap what you sow. Living a little longer has taught me that it is the labor of others that allows each generation the freedom to experience something that the previous generations could have only hoped for. I dedicate my labor to the next generation because my soul understands that we have all benefited from someone else's labor.

ABOUT THE AUTHOR

Chitoka Webb is a successful business owner, motivational speaker, and author who lives in Hendersonville, Tennessee.

Raised by a single mother, Webb grew up in the Preston Taylor housing projects in Nashville and landed her first job in a grocery store at only thirteen years old. When she was a senior in high school, school authorities told her that she couldn't graduate with her class just a week before the ceremony, due to being one point short in her chemistry class. Now, in her mid-thirties, Webb owns several businesses, all of which were founded by her.

Webb began her career as a self-employed entrepreneur at the age of twenty-three. In 1999, she left Nashville and moved to Atlanta, where she nurtured numerous relationships with professional athletes and business leaders while she worked as the only female barber alongside fourteen male barbers. Her highlight moment came during Super Bowl XXXIV when she was invited by her client Anthony Dorsett (son of football great Tony Dorsett) to attend the event as their barber. After great success at this event, she returned to Nashville in pursuit of a dream to open her own barbershop, which she achieved in October 2001. She worked three full-time jobs for three months to make this dream a reality.

After developing two health care agencies and a new, state-of-the-art barbershop, Webb developed Chitoka L. Webb Holdings, Inc., which oversees her professional ventures, and began the early development stages of a foundation that supports her community service projects. During her impressive business growth, Webb suffered blindness for six months as a result of Behcet's disease. High doses of steroidal eye injections and medications corrected her failed eyesight. The Behcet's diagnosis led Webb to write her memoir, *Something Inside of Me.*